T0107211

Pray
Your Way
Through It

Pray
Your Way
Through It

The Inner Meaning
of The Revelation of
St. John the Divine

Joseph Murphy
Ph.D., D.D.

Published 2019 by Gildan Media LLC
aka G&D Media
www.GandDmedia.com

No part of this book may be used, reproduced or transmitted in any manner whatsoever, by any means (electronic, photocopying, recording, or otherwise), without the prior written permission of the author, except in the case of brief quotations embodied in critical articles and reviews. No liability is assumed with respect to the use of the information contained within. Although every precaution has been taken, the author and publisher assume no liability for errors or omissions. Neither is any liability assumed for damages resulting from the use of the information contained herein.

Design by Meghan Day Healey of Story Horse, LLC

Library of Congress Cataloging-in-Publication Data is available upon request

ISBN: 978-1-7225-0135-8

10 9 8 7 6 5 4 3 2 1

Contents

Introduction

This book is based on a series of special lectures and classes given on the inner meaning of *The Revelation of St. John the Divine* in New York, Los Angeles, and other parts of the world. In the second and third centuries there originated a controversy as to the origin of the Book of Revelation. It was claimed that the *Apocalypse* and the Fourth *Gospel* attributed to John were written by Cerinthus, a Gnostic. The critic, Dionysius of Alexandria, declared that the book must have been the work of some John other than the son of Zebedee, arguing from a comparison of the *Apocalypse* on the one hand, and *The Gospel according to John* on the other, regarding style, language, and context.

The Encyclopaedia Biblica points out that *The Gospel according to John, the Epistles,* and *The Apoca-*

lypse all come from the same school, showing linguistic affinities at various points. The consensus of Bible research scholars is that the authorship of *The Revelation* is really unknown, and the claims that it was the work of John are to be discounted. Research into ancient Egyptian manuscripts indicate the possible source of these ancient writings.

There is but one Truth, and all sacred writings are parts or fragments of the ancient wisdom which has come down to us from time immemorial. In the study of comparative religion and sacred writings we must come to the conclusion that a secret, traditional wisdom, an arcane science, underlies all these ancient writings.

In early times this Gnosis, or secret wisdom, was guarded zealously, being imparted only to those deemed worthy of initiation. The Bible is a psychological and spiritual textbook containing the laws of man's mind and the way God works.

The Book of *Revelation* is allegorical and mystical—not historical. We must not construe allegory as history. People have tried in vain to give the *Apocalypse* an historical interpretation; others have looked upon it as prophecy predicting world events. The Bible does not deal with predictions of future events such as wars, calamities, destruction of the world, *etc.*

The *Old* and *New Testaments* do not talk about future events and the destiny of nations.

If the Bible taught these things, it would mean that all things are foreordained, predetermined, and that man has no choice, no free will to mold, fashion, and shape his destiny. If the play is all written and you are here to fulfill your role like an actor following the lines of the play, what would be the use of praying, studying the Bible, learning how the subconscious works? *As a man thinketh in his heart, so is he* proves you can change the future by changing your thought and feeling now. It is your belief about yourself and your habitual thinking that make you well or sick, happy or depressed, prosperous or poor.

The subject matter of the Book of *Revelation,* or *Apocalypse* as it often is called, is veiled in symbolic, figurative, and allegorical language. This method was used by all ancient writers of the Bible, who were masters of allegory, in order to preserve and guard the sacred sciences in their true inner meaning from those who would purposely destroy them. Furthermore, they held that those who are morally unworthy should not receive the inner teaching until they had proved themselves worthy to receive it. If the book had been written in clear language and its inner meaning revealed as a great psychological drama taking place in the consciousness of man, it would undoubtedly have been destroyed by the hands of the first great dictator who came along, whether a Nero, a Ghengis Khan, or a Hitler.

Those illumined seers who wrote the Bibles of the world saw through time and space, and knew the importance of preserving the age-old wisdom, concealing it under symbols, numbers, and cryptograms. The Bible is written in code and the key to it has always been known. Any person can study the general principles of symbolism; he can look up the meaning of the various names and words in a good concordance and see for himself the great psychological and spiritual truths which portray the general scheme of Bible allegory. The language of symbols is universal, and this was the way spiritual knowledge was given to people in ancient times. A symbol appeals to the hearts of all men.

We shall now present a great psychological feast of peace, joy, and happiness as we dwell on the spiritual food of the beautiful Book of *Revelation,* which repudiates the conception of an anthropomorphic God, and with beautiful and sublime imagery points the true way to the heart of God. All the Bibles of the world reveal the eternal verities appertaining to the One God, the Father of all. They all bear witness to the Wisdom of God which is imperishable and which has come down through the ages as a priceless heritage of sacred knowledge.

Historically the Bible is of little or no value. Its beauty and strength lies in its presentation of the laws of life and the way of the Spirit. Approach the Bible with understanding and love, wholeheartedly seeking guidance and inspiration, and the Spirit of Truth will lead you into all Truth.

Chapter 1

(1) The Revelation of Jesus Christ, which God gave unto him, to shew unto his servants things which must shortly come to pass; and he sent and signified it by his angel unto his servant John: (2) Who bare record of the word of God, and of the testimony of Jesus Christ, and of all things that he saw. (3) Blessed is he that readeth, and they that hear the words of this prophecy, and keep those things which are written therein: for the time is at hand.

The Revelation of St. John the Divine is a manual of spiritual development teaching the great art of scientific prayer and not, as so many believe, a cryptic prophecy of future world events. The word *Apocalypse,* or *Apocalypsis,* means to unveil, disrobe, reveal, or uncover. *The Revelation of St. John the Divine* means "God revealing Himself as man." If you sit still, relax, let go, and then mentally divest yourself of your body, name, nationality, race, environment, family, *etc.*, what are you? You will say, "I am invisible—mind and spirit." This is what the Book of *Revelation* is talking about. You are really invisible. You cannot see your mind, thoughts, feelings, beliefs, and convictions; neither can you see the feeling of love, faith, joy, or enthusiasm. You are living with your thoughts, dreams, aspirations, longings, and imaginings. You are not living in your body. Your body lives in you as an idea.

The purpose of the *Apocalypse* is to unveil man and reveal to him the Presence of the Indwelling God. This is the magnificent and glorious purpose of this Book of the Bible. In the following pages you will receive all the significant highlights of the principal or key verses as given in my classes and public lectures.

The first verse says, *The Revelation of Jesus Christ which God gave unto him, to shew unto his . . .* The word *Jesus* is an ancient name for the sun, which was a symbol of the Light or the Presence of God within man. In other words *Jesus* means "I Am," or "Pure Being," the ancient name for God. The word *Christ* is a title and means consecrated or anointed. It corresponds to the Hebrew word *Messiah* or *Savior.* The term *Christ* is the Spiritual Truth about any person or thing. Your *I Am* is the *Christ* or the solution to any problem, and when you say, "I Am," you are announcing the Presence of God within you which is your Christ or Savior because your realization of God is your salvation or the solution to your problem. The words *salvation* and *solution* are used synonymously. In the language of the Bible you are Jesus Christ in action when you become aware of the fact that your I AMness is God, and whatever you affix to I AM you become.

Paul says, *Know ye not that Jesus Christ is within you except ye be reprobates?* In psychological language *Jesus Christ* means the harmonious and synchronous interaction of your conscious and subconscious minds. When you unite true ideas with true feeling you are Jesus Christ in action. Your knowledge of the functioning of your own mind is your savior. In other words man himself is his own savior.

To illustrate how you become Jesus Christ in action, I said to a woman who complained about being lonesome to affirm frequently like a lullaby the following: "I am loved, appreciated, and wanted." She repeated this affirmation until her mind was saturated with the truth of that which she affirmed; then the answer came in the form of the ideal companion who harmonized with her in every way, consummating in marriage.

Every faculty of your mind is a servant. Your thoughts, mental pictures, and emotions are your servants. You are in charge, and you can command your thoughts to do your bidding and bring forth your desire. You are John being initiated into the wonders of your Higher Self. The moment you mother any idea or desire it will come forth into manifestation.

For the time is at hand. The time is always at hand; it is now. In God there is no time or space. When you pray you leave time and space and enter Eternity. Your good is this present moment. Spiritual growth has nothing to do with time or space. You can claim love now, peace now, and strength now. God is the Eternal Now. You don't have to wait for peace, wisdom, joy, or a healing. All these qualities of God are within you, and when you claim your good, Spirit will validate it and give to you according to your mental acceptance. Cease postponing your good.

(7) *Behold, he cometh with clouds; and every eye shall see him, and they also which pierced him: and all kindreds of the earth shall wail because of him. Even so, Amen.*

The meaning of this verse is clear. We cannot see the workings of our subconscious mind; it is like a cloud; but when the cloud has become saturated with vapor, precipitation takes place, and we have rain. When your consciousness becomes saturated with the feeling of being what you long to be or when you have reached the point of conviction, your deeper mind will project the answer as a condition, experience, or event. The law is, whatever is impressed on the subconscious mind is expressed on the screen of space.

(8) *I am Alpha and Omega, the beginning and the ending, saith the Lord, which is, and which was, and which is to come, the Almighty.*

I AM or God is the beginning and the end. In simple, everyday language, the beginning of anything is your desire, idea, thought, or purpose; in other words, when you become aware of being or having some desire in your mind, it is called Alpha or the beginning. Your desire is covered with a cloud which means you don't know how to bring it forth. If you will feel within yourself that the God-Wisdom locked in your subconscious mind is at work, it will bring to pass the fulfilment in ways you do not know. Continue to mother this idea with feeling, and you will succeed in impregnating your deeper mind and the answer to your prayer will be precipitated in the same manner that rain falls from the saturated cloud. The beginning is the acorn and the end is the oak, but the plant is already in the seed, and the apple is already in the apple-seed. The beginning is your idea, and the end (Omega) is its manifestation. Your desire, like a seed, has within it its own mathematics and mechanics, and when planted in the receptive area of your mind, it will gestate and grow in the darkness, eventually coming forth into your objective experience. The solution to all your problems comes out of the clouds of your own consciousness.

(9) *I John, who also am your brother, and companion in tribulation; and in the kingdom and patience of Jesus Christ, was in the isle that is called Patmos, for the word of God, and for the testimony of Jesus Christ.*

John is the type of mind that is always transcending itself, the man who is constantly giving birth to spiritual values. *Tribulation* means suffering; actually your desire is your tribulation, because if you realized your desire, you would not be suffering. There is no occasion to suffer when we release our vain opinions and false beliefs and enthrone in our mind the spiritual truths about our mind and the way it works. *To suffer* also means to allow, as to suffer it to be done now. *Tribulation* means to undergo a change whereby we separate ourselves from that which binds, restricts, or inhibits us.

There are birth pangs in the change because before something is born something must die, before something is created something must be destroyed. When you pray about a situation or condition you will oftentimes find that things get worse before the answer comes; this is a cleansing process whereby the old state disintegrates, creating some pain and tribulation such as confusion; but this is a good sign

as it indicates the new state is being born. It is somewhat similar to spring cleaning when the mistress of
the house creates a lot of dust during the cleaning
process.

The *isle of Patmos* means to still your mind and
dwell mentally on God. You are then in an island sur-
rounded by water, *i.e.,* you have a firm conviction and
faith in God which remains unmoved and unyielding.
You are fixed in the belief that what you now contemplate in the secret place of your mind will come to
pass, knowing in your heart that it is done unto you
as you believe. Your emotions are stilled because you
are resting in abiding faith and trust in mental and
spiritual laws which transcend all conditions, circumstances, and external appearances.

You are in the *isle of Patmos* when you shut the
door of your five senses, turn within to God, and
claim that the God who gave you your desire or idea is
the same God who fulfills it. Sense and feel the reality of your desire and rejoice in its fulfillment. You
can believe in the reality of your idea just as surely as
you can believe you have a hand or a heart. Thoughts
are things, ideas execute themselves, what we feel we
attract, and what we contemplate we become. When
we know these simple truths and their corollaries, we
can go to the *isle of Patmos* in faith and confidence and
become firm in our conviction that what we pray for

already subsists in Infinite Mind and may be said to exist when we feel its reality in our hearts.

(10) *I was in the Spirit on the Lord's day, and heard behind me a great voice, as of a trumpet, (11) Saying, I am Alpha and Omega, the first and the last: and, What thou seest, write in a book, and send it unto the seven churches which are in Asia; unto Ephesus and unto Smyrna, and unto Pergamos, and unto Thyatira, and unto Sardis, and unto Philadelphia, and unto Laodicea.*

The day of the Lord is when the Light and Intelligence of God shines in your mind, when you know that your own consciousness is God, and that It is the only Creative Power in your world. *Spirit* means feeling, an animation on the inside, and enthusiasm. You are *in the Spirit* when you think of God as the faceless, formless, boundless Awareness within you, knowing that He is the Only Presence and the Only Power. Do not strain for a realization, but simply feel this great Truth. If you are praying about a particular problem, enter into the *Spirit* or feeling of the joy of the answered prayer. The *voice* that you hear which seems like a trumpet is the sound of your answered prayer. It also represents the voice of intuition, and means taught from within. Sometimes the idea or perfect answer wells up spontaneously in your mind like toast out of a toaster.

In verse eleven the *book* spoken of is your subconscious mind in which you are always inscribing your habitual thoughts, feelings, beliefs, and reactions to life. Whatever you feel as true on the inside, you experience on the outside. The subjective mind receives impressions from our conscious mind which is the scribe, and the ideas impressed thereon become form, function, and experience. *Asia* means the East, the dawn, the within, the hidden, the spiritual realm. It means the Spirit within, your awareness of the Indwelling Divine Presence which is represented by the rising sun in Eastern symbology. All religions have their first impetus in Asia and represent the Infinite Intelligence and Wisdom of God resident in the unconscious of all men.

Before we elaborate on the meaning of the *seven churches*, we must understand the meaning of the word *church*. The true *church* is the consciousness of man from which he draws out all the wisdom, strength, and power he needs to maintain himself fully and be expressed at his highest level. A church in Bible language is not a sect or denomination. It is an aggregation of spiritual ideas in individual consciousness.

To send a message to the seven churches a new state of consciousness or mental attitude must be formed. Man must gain an understanding of God as Spirit and establish friendly and harmonious relations to Spirit. The *church* of God is a mental and spiritual awareness of the Truths of God which are gradually absorbed into the mentality. You are building the church of God on earth when you begin a silent, interior planting of spiritual concepts, which work like leaven and in due season transform your whole life.

Countless millions read the Bible according to the letter instead of the spirit or underlying meaning. The various forms, creeds, ceremonies, liturgies, and rituals are all symbolic of inner processes of spiritual growth and awareness. Your *church* is your Deeper Self from which you extract the Wisdom, Power, and Glory of God embedded therein. Remember that a *church* is not made of creeds or forms; neither is it contained in walls of marble and brick. The highest altar in the land is the purified heart of man. Each man is the temple of the Living God, and the Spirit of Truth will lead and guide all men to the Everlasting Truth which is One and Indivisible. One God, One Law, One Life, One Truth, One Eternal, One Father of all—God. All men who walk the earth have the marvelous opportunity to turn to the God-Presence within for light and inspiration, and each shall receive. When all men make a habit of doing this, the real *Church* of God will be found where it always was—in the heart of man.

The seven churches are the seven steps or degrees of awareness through which all of us go before reaching the point of mental conviction or internal, vivid realization concerning the subject or condition about which we are praying. When we have reached the point of fulfillment mentally and emotionally where there is no longer any quarrel with the conscious or subconscious mind, we no longer feel any need or inclination to pray further. We are satisfied and have that inner, silent knowing of the soul that all is well. It is a deep, inner feeling of certitude whereby you know that you know. You bless the situation at this point and leave it. You have affirmed the Truth and spoken the word which will not return unto you void. You are now resting in the unalterable conviction that your prayer is already answered in Divine Mind, and the moment you think not, it shall appear on the screen of space.

The seven churches represent the seven days of creation, which again represent the length of time it takes you to get an answer to your prayer. If you have an instantaneous healing or demonstration the seven days or seven stages of mental and spiritual development have been traversed. *And God blessed the seventh day and sanctified it.* (GEN. 2:3)

According to some geologists the earth beneath our feet bears record of six great creative periods, with a seventh process still functioning and in the process of completion. There are seven colors of the spectrum, seven principal tones of music, seven senses of man; the numeral seven represents fulness or a completed

state. *The seven churches* also refer to the Sabbath
Day. The *Sabbath* means the seventh day, seventh
month, restoration, at-one-ment, completion, perfection, wholeness, repose, and rest. *The seven churches*
or *the Sabbath Day* represent a state of mind that man
enters or acquires when he goes into the silence of the
soul, into communion with God where he finds true
rest and peace. The seven churches represent also the
seventh or perfect stage of one's spiritual unfoldment.
You can send your message to the seven churches
within you at any hour. Drop your ideal with feeling
into your subconscious mind, and you will come to
the seventh stage.

The following are the stages or steps you go
through before any prayer is answered:

1. *Ephesus* means desire, plan, or purpose.
2. *Smyrna* means fragrance.
3. *Pergamos* means strongly united, closely knit.
4. *Thyatira* means incense, inspired zeal.
5. *Sardis* means precious stone, joy.
6. *Philadelphia* means fraternal love.
7. *Laodicea* means judgment, detachment.

The *seven churches* are seven states of consciousness.
You send your message to the seven churches this
way: You go to the isle of Patmos within yourself,

which is your own mind, where you contemplate God and pass through seven degrees of awareness to the conditioned state. First you have a desire. Then you dwell in the fragrant state which is the thrill of being or having what you want through the Power of God. In the third step, you mentally and emotionally unite with your ideal or desire by exalting it, lifting it up in mind, wooing it, and embracing it.

The fourth step, represented by incense, is sustained thanksgiving, thanking God for the gift already received. You are thankful in the same way as though you were thanking a man in a store for the fur coat he is going to send you to your home. You trust him implicitly. You have not yet received the coat, but you know you will. Your father promised you a car for graduation; you have not yet received it, but you remember the joy, the thrill, the incense burning within your heart when he promised it to you. All you had was a promise, but you were just as happy as though you had received it because you knew from previous experience that your father always kept his word. Can't you offer the incense of thankfulness to God who never fails? His promises are based on Law, and He has already given you everything. He is within you. Your uplifted and grateful heart will work miracles. Never cease offering incense on the altar of your heart to God Who gave you all things.

The fifth step follows which is a joyous reaction where you are bubbling over with a joyous expectancy, knowing what you claimed in the silence on the isle of Patmos will come to pass, as Spirit always validates and makes good your claim or belief. The sixth step is Love or at-one-ment with your ideal which represents identification. You are now one with your desire. Your subconscious has absorbed it, and you are filled full— there has been a marriage of the idea and feeling. You have mentally absorbed your desire in the same manner as a piece of bread becomes tissue, muscle, bone, and blood stream.

The last or final step is *Laodicea* which is a rest in God—the creative act is finished. Having done all, you stand on the word of Truth. There is always an interval of time between the impregnation of the subconscious and the manifestation. This period is called the stillness, the Sabbath, the seventh day, the seventh hour—all of which mean subconscious pregnancy. Your subconscious is having a child, which child shall be born at the right time in the right way according to the wisdom of the subconscious. One problem may be solved in an hour, another in a week or a month, another in minutes. Some magnificent demonstrations or answers to prayer have taken years as we count them on the three dimensional plane of life; but in all cases the message to the seven churches or the seven degrees of unfoldment were gone through.

(12) *And I turned to see the voice that spake with me. And being turned, I saw seven golden candlesticks;* (13) *And in the midst of the seven candlesticks one like unto the Son of man, clothed with a garment down to the foot, and girt about the paps with a golden girdle.* The *seven candlesticks* are the seven churches. The *garment* which you wear is your mood, your feeling, your joyous conviction. You have been to the banquet table of God where you come mentally clothed in the garment of love, forgiveness, peace, joy, and good will. When you enter into a great psychological feast of joy and happiness, you are wearing the garment of love and you are wearing, symbolically speaking, the *golden girdle* which is a symbol of joy.

When you pray, you must always go to the God-Presence wearing a golden robe or a clean heart and mind free from resentment, ill will, hostility, prejudice, or condemnation. These attitudes of mind preclude and obstruct the flow of the Divine Healing Presence. The debris must be removed from the pipe before the water will flow through freely. Likewise a contaminated consciousness must be cleansed of all perverted and noxious feelings in order for harmony, health, and peace to enter in.

(14) *His head and his hairs were white like wool, as white as snow; and his eyes were as a flame of fire; (15) And his feet like unto fine brass, as if they burned in a furnace; and his voice as the sound of many waters.*

The *head* and *hairs* mentioned here represent the intellect anointed by the Wisdom of God. *Hairs* represent the Power and Wisdom of God. *Head* symbolizes the intellect or conscious mind. When your thoughts are God's thoughts, God's Power is with your thought of good. When you have a clean mind and a clean heart, or a true God-like idea and the true feeling which follows, your mind is referred to as *white as wool or snow.*

In verse fifteen the word *feet* means understanding. *Brass* is an alloy formed by the union of zinc and copper, which means a union of your desire and feeling, your mind and your heart. Your understanding consists of your knowledge of the working of your mind enabling you to unite with what you want and to feel yourself to be what you want to be.

(16) *And he had in his right hand seven stars: and out of his mouth went a sharp twoedged sword: and his countenance was as the sun shineth in his strength.*

The *twoedged sword* coming *out of his mouth* means out of your mouth or mind comes speech, or comes a voice, which is vibration. Truth is a *sword* because it severs us from our old, false beliefs and negative patterns, creating a quarrel in our mind in order to resolve a problem. Remember also that whatever you think and feel about another you are creating in your own experience for the simple reason that what you think and feel you create. Truth is a *twoedged sword* in the sense that it is the subjective factor which is always the determining factor. What you believe you create. Man is belief expressed.

When you perceive the Truth of Being, you will believe only in the Goodness and Love of God and expect only the best. You can then roam the whole world wearing the garment of God, and the whole world will be blessed because you walked this way. When you enthrone a God of Love in your mind and believe in your heart that God is the Great, Beneficent Father, you will get a response from the Father of Light as love, peace, guidance, abundance, and security. He will turn to you as you turn to Him. God is to you what you believe Him to be.

(17) *And when I saw him, I fell at his feet as dead. And he laid his right hand upon me, saying unto me, Fear not; I am the first and the last: (18) I am he that liveth, and was dead; and, behold, I am alive for evermore, Amen; and have the keys of hell and of death.*

Verse seventeen means that when you perceive the Creative Power within you, you become as *dead*; *i.e.,* asleep to the world and alive to God. You realize once

and for all the beginning and the end are the same—
the thought and the thing, the idea and its manifestation, the oak and the acorn are one. The flower and
the seed are one. Your desire and its manifestation are
one in your mind. All things subsist in Divine Mind.
Alpha is the desire and *Omega* is the manifestation of
the desire. God gave you the desire, God will fulfill
the desire, and God will reveal to you every step necessary for its unfoldment. The place of fulfillment is
in your mind, and the place of origin is your mind.

Consciousness is always dying and giving birth to
something new. You can die to poverty by claiming
God's Opulence is flowing through you. As you continue to do this, the poverty state will be starved to
death and you give birth to the prosperity consciousness. The old man is dead, and we now see another
man rolling in wealth. You can die to fear and live in
faith in God. You can die to ill will and feast on good
will. You can die to sickness by taking your attention
away from what you do not want and placing all your
attention on God and His Infinite Healing Presence,
claiming that what is true of God is true of you. The
keys of hell and death mean your capacity to die to the
old state and live in the new. I must die to what I am
before I can live to that which I long to be.

(19) *Write the things which thou hast seen, and the
things which are, and the things which shall be hereafter;*

(20) *The mystery of the seven stars which thou sawest in my right hand, and the seven golden candlesticks. The seven stars are the angels of the seven churches: and the seven candlesticks which thou sawest are the seven churches.*

The *seven stars* and the *angels of the seven churches* are the same thing. An *angel* is a messenger of God, a new idea, a new attitude, a new interpretation of life. The *angel* must come before you can change. You can't change your old ways of thinking until you get a new idea. You come to new judgments, decisions, and conclusions when you learn the Creative Power of your own mind. To realize that what you imagine and feel you create is to experience a visitation of an angel. This angel or new idea heralds the birth of your savior or solution to your problem.

As you walk in the mood or feeling that your prayer is being answered, in the same way the sun will be resurrected in the morning; you will have found your savior; then the dawn will appear and all the shadows will flee.

Chapter 2

We have already elaborated on the meaning of *angel*, the *seven churches*, and the *seven candlesticks*. Since we plan to avoid as much repetition as possible in this book, we will start therefore with the third and fourth verses, avoiding material already covered. The *seven stars* as outlined previously are the seven degrees of awareness through which we go before becoming subjectively one with our desire.

(3) *And hast borne, and has patience, and for my name's sake hast laboured, and hast not fainted. (4) Nevertheless I have somewhat against thee, because thou hast left thy first love.*

Your *first love* is God or the Spirit within. When you are loyal and devoted to the One Power recognizing no other, you are loving God. The moment you give power to fear, doubt, or external phenomena, you have left your *first love* and will find yourself in trouble. It means you have wandered away on the periphery of life worshipping all sorts of strange gods. Now you must return to the Center where God dwells in Peace and Harmony, and here be refreshed and replenished from the standpoint of Truth. Here in the silence in communion with God, you can receive Guidance, Strength, and Power to solve all your problems and rise triumphant over all difficulties.

Many scientists have discovered the secret of drawing wisdom from the Deeper Self. Poincare, the French mathematician, would relax, let go, and get passive and still; then he would turn over his mathematical problem to his Deeper Mind which knew the answer. He turned his request over with faith and confidence—this activated the wisdom in his subjective mind, and when his conscious mind was preoccupied with other things, the answer invariably came to his surface mind in a manner similar to toast popping out of the toaster.

(5) *Remember therefore from whence thou art fallen, and repent, and do the first works; or else I will come unto thee quickly, and will remove thy candlestick out of his place, except thou repent.*

In verse five the word *repent* means to think in a new way and to get a new idea. When you get a new idea about the creative power of your mind, you begin to think in a new way, and as you think and feel so do you become. Thought and feeling create your destiny, and when you begin to think right, feel right, act right, and do right, you are really repenting. To *do the first works* means that when a desire comes to us, we must not stay with our limitations. We must plant our seed in the subjective mind and must give it our full attention. Clarify your desire, define your goal, and be definite and purposeful—this is the job of *Ephesus*. When you know what you want and have defined it clearly in your conscious mind, you will always receive a response from your subconscious mind, which is full of wisdom and intelligence and knows how to bring it to pass.

(6) *But this thou hast, that thou hatest the deeds of the Nicolaitanes, which I also hate.* (7) *He that hath an ear, let him hear what the Spirit saith unto the churches; To him that overcometh will I give to eat of the tree of life, which is in the midst of the paradise of God.*

The *deeds of the Nicolaitanes* refer to phallic worship, which is an abomination of the Law. The deeds of the Nicolaitanes are likened to the actions of Balaam, meaning fornication or cohabiting with evil and destructive thoughts in our mind. To *hate* in the Bible is to completely reject anything negative or destructive in our mind. If we enthrone error in our mind, we will be compelled to express evil. We leave our *first* love which is God whenever we indulge in bitterness, prejudice, hatred, or negation of any kind.

We *eat of the tree of life* spoken of in verse seven when we meditate or mentally feast on something elevating, dignifying, and praiseworthy. The *tree of life* is the Presence of God within you. It is the Christmas tree, and all fruits are hanging on it. Everything you are seeking is within you. No matter what the problem may be, the answer is within you.

A woman who attended the class on *Revelation* had ears which heard the Truth of God—her mind was open and receptive to new ideas. Her child was very ill, and hope of saving the child's life was given up by all except the mother. She sat by the bed in the hospital and prayed as follows: "God is the Life of my child, and His Healing Power is flowing through every atom of his being. The Peace of God floods his mind and body, and through His Power my child is made whole." She silently repeated this simple prayer over and over again trying to lift up the idea of health in her mind. She knew intuitively and instinctively as she continued praying that she would reach the point of inner peace about her boy. After a few hours the child began to cry for food. The doctor examined the child and said he had passed the crisis. She had practiced sending a message to the seven churches, which meant that she had raised her idea in consciousness through seven degrees of awareness or feeling until an inner conviction took over.

We will go over these seven steps briefly again. *Ephesus* means your desire, which we realize comes from God reminding us of a void in our life. *Smyrna* means hearing; we discipline ourselves so that we hear or give attention only to that which will bless and heal us. We listen to the good news within ourselves—this is the fragrant state *Pergamos,* where we come to the point of clear-cut decision in our mind whereby we know the Deeper Mind responds to our definite decision and trust in It. There is no doubt in our minds. *Thyatira* is the state where we feel the joy of what we are contemplating, when we see and feel the happy ending. *Sardis* is where we mentally come to the place of rest or conviction. *Philadelphia* is where we love our conviction and adhere to it faithfully. Laodicea is detachment where we rest in God. Impregnation of the subconscious has taken place, and in a little while the answer to our prayer will be made manifest. These are stages we go through mentally whether our prayer is answered in a minute, an hour, a month, or a year.

(8) *And unto the angel of the church in Smyrna write; These things saith the first and the last, which was dead, and is alive;* (9) *I know thy works, and tribulation, and poverty (but thou art rich) and I know the blasphemy of*

them which say they are Jews, and are not, but are the synagogue of Satan.

A *Jew* is a person whose intellect is illumined by the Wisdom of God; he knows the Law of Life and follows It. Many people say they believe in God, and at the same time they postulate another power called "Satan" or the "Devil"—this is *blasphemy,* and their *synagogue* or mind becomes double-minded and confused. To say, "I believe God is Love," and then to hate someone is a contradiction in the mind. To say, "I believe God is the Source of all blessings and the Supreme Cause," and at the same time to be angry and resentful toward others, blaming them for your loss or trouble, is to cohabit with evil and false beliefs in your mind.

Satan means a lier in wait, an adversary, a false belief, hater, accuser, opposer, or contradictor. Any idea you entertain in your mind which opposes the Truth about God is *Satan.* Self-depreciation and self-condemnation admit the accuser, which is a destructive thought in your own mind admitted there by you and entertained in your mental realm. There is no law which says that you have to entertain a gangster, assassin, marauder, or intruder in your mind. Such negative thoughts will rob you of peace, harmony, health, vitality, and enthusiasm, and leave you a mental and physical wreck. The *Satanic* thought is any suggestion or idea that tends to persuade you to turn away from the belief in One Power and One Cause. *I beheld Satan as lightning fall from heaven.* (LUKE 10:18.)

Heaven is your mind at peace relatively speaking. When you permit the thoughts of fear, hate, jealousy, *etc.,* into your mind, there are Satan and war in heaven. When you affirm the Truth of Being, erroneous thought falls away; that is, Satan falls from heaven as lightning. Ultimately all evil destroys itself. *Salvation is of the Jews*—that is to say the solution or the answer to prayer comes to the man who is consciously aware of the Indwelling God and His responsiveness; he is the type of man who knows that what he consciously desires to be, to do, or to have, will get a response from the Deeper Mind full of Wisdom, Power, and Intelligence.

The *synagogue of Satan* represents the accumulation or aggregation of negative thoughts in the mind. The *congregation* represents thoughts, feelings, opinions, and beliefs. If a man says he is a Jew, and is bringing forth misery, pain, sickness, and lack, in Bible language he is not a Jew but belongs to the *synagogue of Satan,* which is a false belief about God, life, the universe, and all things good. He believes in misfortune instead of good fortune. We are not *Jews* if we are not demonstrating harmony, health, peace, joy, and abundance. Some people say, "I believe that God can do all things;" then they say, "My child has no chance, it is going to die." They are actually saying that the Creative Intelligence which made the body cannot heal, thereby denying the Presence and Power of God.

(10) *Fear none of those things which thou shalt suffer: behold, the devil shall cast some of you into prison, that ye may be tried: and ye shall have tribulation ten days: be thou faithful unto death, and I will give thee a crown of life. (11) He that hath an ear, let him hear what the Spirit saith unto the churches; He that overcometh shall not be hurt of the second death.*

In prayer we must be *faithful unto death*; the death of the old state takes place as we remain faithful to our ideal or desire every step of the way. In prayer we must give allegiance to the One Power, and as we give devotion, faith, and allegiance to our desire, the old condition will disappear and the new state will be resurrected. The *crown* we receive is victory, triumph, and accomplishment. We become victorious over problems as we remain faithful to our vision or goal, knowing in our heart that no matter how black the tunnel is, we shall come out into the light.

The meaning of verse eleven can be explained this way: The first death is the Universal Life or God assuming the form of the child born into the world— this is the Formless assuming form or Life becoming manifest. The first resurrection takes place when we awaken to the realization that our Consciousness or Awareness is God; we learn to resurrect the Wisdom, Intelligence, and Power of God within ourselves. We transform our lives and environment as we learn that whatever concept we engage in and give attention to in our mind, we create. In other words we learn the Law of Creative Mind; then comes the manifestation of our hopes, wishes, and aspirations. The *second death* takes place when we begin to lose our limitations and start dying to fear, ignorance, superstition, and error of all kinds, thereby resurrecting faith, love, joy, happiness, and confidence in an Everlasting Principle which never changes.

The *ten days* spoken of in verse ten means the length of time it takes us to bring about an agreement between our conscious and subconscious mind. In the numeral ten, the one means the male element or our idea or desire, and the zero means the womb or female capacity in all of us, the feeling or emotional nature. When we emotionalize the idea, creation has taken place, the male and female are fused into one, and God has entered in; *i.e.*, the Creative Power of God is made manifest in such a union, and the result comes forth which is the answer to our prayer. *If two of you shall agree on earth as touching any thing that they shall ask, it shall be done for them of my Father which is in heaven.* (MATT. 18:19.)

(12) And to the angel of the church in Pergamos write; These things saith he which hath the sharp sword with two edges; (13) I know thy works, and where thou dwellest, even where Satan's seat is: and thou holdest fast my name, and hast not denied my faith, even in those days wherein Antipas was my faithful martyr, who was slain among you, where Satan dwelleth.

The *sharp word* means that a sword cuts, which means we sever ourselves from our old concepts of limitation and come to the place of decision in our mind where Truth prevails in all its pristine glory. We martyr *Antipas*, which means second sight or intuition, when we become negative and resist evil. *Resist not him that is evil.* (MATT. 5:39.) We do not need to resist evil or Satan since it has no power of itself. By remaining positive to the Truths of God all error will fall away from our life. The resistant attitude of mind leads to martyrdom of the Inner Wisdom, symbolically speaking, for the Wisdom of the Subjective Self does not rise to the surface mind when it is disturbed and confused.

(17) He that hath an ear, let him hear what the Spirit saith unto the churches; To him that overcometh will I give to eat of the hidden manna, and will give him a white stone, and in the stone a new name written, which no man knoweth saving he that receiveth it.

The word *manna* is a symbol of Goodness and Truth which feeds the soul. There is a Spiritual

Wisdom which wells up from the subjective depths within those who sincerely seek It and which waters and refreshes the mind and puts sweetness into the mouth. *Manna* is an outpouring of Divine Wisdom which fills the soul with joy. *Manna* is the bread of peace, joy, love, faith, and confidence in God. It is the blessed bread of God which we partake of when we meditate on the Truth of God.

The *white stone* is the purified or cleansed mind which follows our feasting on God and His blessed qualities. We write *a new name* or nature because we are absolutely convinced of God's Goodness and Love. As we go on a great, psychological feast of peace and happiness we make a deep impression which is indelibly engraved in consciousness, and our whole nature is transformed. Man becomes what he contemplates; knowing this anyone can write what they wish in their subconscious mind, for whatever we feel as true will come to pass. No one can ever take away this inner experience from you because you have tasted God and found Him Good. No one can give this experience to you—you must receive it yourself.

(20) *Notwithstanding I have a few things against thee, because thou sufferest that woman Jezebel, which calleth herself a prophetess, to teach and to seduce my servants to commit fornication, and to eat things sacrificed unto idols.*

Our moods, feelings, and beliefs *prophesy* or determine that which is to come. Man with the conviction of God's Love in his heart prophesies the Good only because he knows that his faith in God and all things is his fortune. Man's present mood or mental attitude is a *prophecy* of that which is to come. When man permits his five senses to run wild, and mentally and emotionally unites or cohabits with evil in his mind, he is *fornicating*, in Bible language. This is referred to as being *seduced by the prophetess Jezebel*. Every man must be a prophet of God and reproduce the qualities, attributes, and potencies of God here and now.

(22) Behold, I will cast her into a bed, and them that commit adultery with her into great tribulation, except they repent of their deeds.

We commit *adultery* when we hate, resent, or indulge in self-criticism and self-pity. If we give power to stars, to the weather, to people, and to entities, we are *committing adultery* because we are uniting mentally and emotionally with false beliefs. Actually we are creating idols in our mind. *Adultery* and *idolatry* are used synonymously.

(23) And I will kill her children with death; and all the churches shall know that I am he which searched the reins and hearts; and I will give unto every one of you according to your works.

The *children* of negative thoughts and emotions are sickness, lack, frustration, and limitation of all kinds. To permit fear, hate, or ill will to browbeat, intimidate, bully, and frighten us is to cohabit with evil in the bed of our mind. Our subconscious mind will always express what we have impressed upon it—good if good, evil if evil. No matter what we claim or affirm with the lips, our real feelings and beliefs are always made manifest. The Bible says adultery is of the heart—the *heart* means your emotional and feeling nature, your subconscious mind. The body does nothing of itself—the body moves as it is moved upon, the body acts as it is acted upon.

(26) *And he that overcometh, and keepeth my works unto the end, to him will I give power over the nations: (23) And I will give him the morning star.*

The *morning star* is your recognition of the Presence and Power of God within you. On the heels of this discovery will come your birthday in God. The *morning star* heralds the dawning of the new day, proclaiming the resurrection of the sun, which bathes the world in beauty and redeems it from darkness and death. Your conviction that the Almighty Power of God is now going before you in majesty and might, and always is moving on your behalf; it will make all your dreams come true. You will find that all your ways are pleasantness and all your paths are peace.

Chapter 3

We are taking the key verses of this chapter and again avoiding interpretations previously given.

(5) *He that overcometh, the same shall be clothed in white raiment; and I will not blot out his name out of the book of life, but I will confess his name before my Father, and before his angels.*

The term *white raiment* means a purified state of consciousness, a clean mind free from guilt, fear, ill will, *etc.* The *book of life* is your subconscious mind, in which all your reactions, feelings, and beliefs are deposited morning, noon, and night. Your subconscious mind is like a recording machine. It records all your moods, sensations, and reactions of the day. The wise man sees to it that he records in the *book of life* strong, powerful, loving, and harmonious convictions about the constructive values of life.

(7) And to the angel of the church in Philadelphia write; These things saith he that is holy, he that is true, he that hath the key of David, he that openeth, and no man shutteth; and shutteth, and no man openeth; (8) I know thy works: behold, I have set before thee an open door, and no man can shut it: for thou hast a little strength, and hast kept my word, and has not denied my name. (9) Behold, I will make them of the synagogue of Satan, which say they are Jews, and are not, but do lie; behold, I will make them to come and worship before thy feet, and to know that I have loved thee.

David represents Divine Love individualized in man's consciousness. The *key of David* is the consciousness of God's Love abiding in your heart which melts everything unlike itself. A man in our class on the book of *Revelation* told me that he had lost $20,000 in a business venture; it was a complete loss. He listened to the meaning of verse eight and said to himself, "How can I capitalize on my loss?" He assumed a positive attitude and affirmed boldly, "Infinite Intelligence is opening up a new door of expression for me, and I follow the guidance and direction which comes to me." A new idea came to him after a few days. His father-in-law backed him in the same business, and applying the new idea to his business he has gone ahead in a wonderful way. He profited from his mistake and capitalized on his business misfortune.

The term *Jew* in verse nine has been previously explained. You are a *Jew* when you are releasing your hidden powers and filling each day with finer experiences in love and life.

(12) *Him that overcometh will I make a pillar in the temple of my God, and he shall go no more out; and I will write upon him the name of my God, and the name of the city of my God, which is new Jerusalem, which cometh down out of heaven from my God: and I will write upon him my new name.*

The real test of true faith and confidence is what man does under pressure, or when he comes face to face with a seemingly impossible situation. The tendency of many is to run away, give up, and surrender. There is only one way to face any problem, and that is as a champion. You can overcome all difficulties through the Power and Wisdom of God. To know this is to instill courage and faith into your life. Never permit an obstacle, setback, or disappointment to stop you. As you keep on picturing the harmonious solution, the happy ending, knowing an Almighty Power is backing you up, you will reach a point of inner conviction which is the *pillar in the temple of God*. A *pillar* means a fixed, immovable state of mind, meaning your absolute faith in God's Law and in His answer to your prayer. You *go no more out* in the sense that you no longer seek for that which you have. When you reach the point of inner certitude, there is nothing more to be done. You have written a *new name,* a new estimate, or blueprint of yourself in your Deeper Mind. You change your *name* when you begin to act upon your knowledge of the Spirit within you, bringing forth Love, Peace, Joy, and Happiness.

(15) *I know thy works, that thou art neither cold nor hot: I would thou wert cold or hot.*

This verse is very important because it points out that we must cease to vacillate, waiver, quiver, and hesitate, but rather come to a clear-cut and definite decision that there is but One Supreme Power which is a God of Love, forever seeking to express through us. Many people become enthusiastic for a while about the creative power of thought; then they disappear until the next problem. Others say, "It is nice to hear," and they never do anything with the Truths they hear. Others say, "O, this thing doesn't work; I've tried it."

When we try to mix the old ideas with the new concept of God and His Laws, we get nowhere and become lukewarm. We must become enthusiastic about new interpretation of Life. We must give our allegiance completely to the Supreme Power within, and rejoice that we have discovered the power of our thought to bring us health or sickness, peace or sorrow, wealth or poverty. We must be glad to work *with* our subconscious, not *against* it. We certainly should be thrilled to know the way the mind works and begin now to convey to our subconscious mind dynamic, loving, positive, and highly productive thoughts and mental imagery. There should not be one moment's hesitation about making up our mind.

(18) *I counsel thee to buy of me gold tried in the fire, that thou mayest be rich; and white raiment, that thou mayest be clothed, and that the shame of thy nakedness do not appear; and anoint thin eyes with eyesalve, that thou mayest see.*

The *gold* mentioned is the Power of God in action in your life. To *anoint your eyes with eyesalve* means to develop your intuitive faculties, sometimes called the *third eye*. There are extra-sensory powers in all of us, and you can get guidance and illumination on any subject. In developing intuition you must never use force or mental coercion. Banish all anxiety and tension. The latter means you are full of fear, and such an attitude prevents the Wisdom of God from rising to the surface mind as a feeling, hunch, intimation, urge, or premonition. Your intuitive voice, if you welcome it with faith and confidence, gives you a strong feeling to do this or that, or to make a certain contract. When you pray for guidance, a lead will come. You must recognize that lead and follow it. Train yourself immediately to listen to your intuition and respond to its inner push, and you will greatly enhance your success along all lines of endeavor. You will grow to recognize the inner Voice by experience, trusting in God at all times to lead and guide you.

Let me illustrate how intuition works. A minister friend of mine asked me whether I thought the church he directed should purchase another church property which was being vacated. I said to him, "Let's pray about it and follow the lead that comes." Nothing happened for a few days; then he phoned me saying they were having a board meeting to decide whether to purchase or not. While he was talking I could "feel" that the answer was "No," and he said, "You know, I feel the answer is "No." Subsequent events proved that he was right.

Your intuition works—*if* you give it the opportunity to respond by maintaining a positive, receptive attitude of mind. You must never try to force your own opinions or influence the intuitive urge in any way. In developing intuition you use reason and logic as far as they go; then you turn the request over to the deeper mind with faith and confidence, knowing in your heart that the answer always comes. You will recognize the answer by an overpowering hunch or feeling, a silent inner knowing of the soul, and by a sense of inner certitude.

(20) *Behold, I stand at the door, and knock: if any man hear my voice, and open the door, I will come in to him, and will sup with him, and he with me.*

God is always *knocking* at the *door* of your heart as a desire. If you *open the door,* which means if you welcome the desire in your mind and treat it cordially and lovingly, you will succeed in becoming one with it mentally and emotionally. You are *supping* with your desire when you feast with joy on the reality of your desire. The Healing Presence is always knocking at your door, and if you will open your mind and heart, and listen to the Voice of Truth, you will have a perfect healing.

A man in one of our classes on the Bible told me that his little boy's finger was twisted in an accident. Every night he would picture a perfect finger on his boy's hand, claiming that there was a perfect idea of a finger in the Mind of God. Prior to falling asleep he would hear his son say to him joyously, "Daddy, look at my finger, it is perfect!" In a month's time the boy's finger was perfectly straight.

Remember the Spirit is always knocking at the door, and the latch opens from the inside. We turn the Holy Visitor away every time that we cease to have faith and confidence in the Spiritual Power as Supreme and Sovereign. If we give power to other things, to people, to conditions, and to circumstances, we are turning the Visitor away. If we say, "I can't," or "I'm incurable," we are actually rejecting the God-Presence which comes to us as a desire for perfect health and harmony. We always know whether or not we have let the Holy Visitor into our heart, by our attitude, demeanor, poise, and balance.

A radio listener wrote saying that one of her tenants was boisterous, rude, noisy, and had drunken brawls in the apartment, annoying all the other tenants. He refused to leave. She stilled her mind, listened to the soft tread of the Unseen Guest, and bid Him welcome. She said that the thoughts in her mind that were intimidating and browbeating her left her completely as she turned to the Spirit within. She decreed that the Presence of God was where this tenant was and that he was in his true place, releasing him completely to the ocean of Infinite Love. She prayed in this manner until she got the reaction which satisfied, which means inner peace and tranquillity. The man paid up his rent, left quietly and she attracted a very spiritually-minded tenant.

Chapter 4

(1) After this I looked, and, behold, a door was opened in heaven: and the first voice which I heard was as it were of a trumpet talking with me; which said, Come up hither, and I will shew thee things which must be hereafter. (2) And immediately I was in the spirit: and, behold, a throne was set in heaven, and one sat on the throne. (3) And he that sat was to look upon like a jasper and a sardine stone: and there was a rainbow round about the throne, in sight like unto an emerald. (4) And round about the throne were four and twenty seats: and upon the seats I saw four and twenty elders sitting, clothed in white raiment; and they had on their heads crowns of gold.

This is a wonderful chapter on meditation. When we close our eyes, still the mind, and think of the Infinite Healing Presence within, we are absent from the body (problems, difficulties, sickness, *etc.*,) and we are present with our Lord as we contemplate the solution to our problems through the Wisdom and Power of God. We have shut the door of the senses upon the outside world, and we have opened another door to the inside, to the subjective realm, into *heaven*. The *trumpet* which you hear represents your inner tone, mood, or feeling which becomes exhilarating, elevating, and inspiring as you contemplate your good. This is the *voice of the trumpet*. Your faith and conviction is a prophecy of that which is to come.

I will shew these things which must be hereafter means that in meditation you can have a preview of things to come, you can see the answer to your prayer before you experience it objectively. In prayer you call things that be not, as though they were, and the unseen becomes seen.

I explained these verses in our class on *Revelation*, and a young actress, who said she had reached the end of her rope, experimented during the prayer period as follows: She began to picture a contract in her hand; she began to feel it and give thanks, saying to herself, "It's mine now. I have so much to give." She lived with the mental picture of acceptance knowing that having seen and felt its reality in her mind, she would experience it objectively. She received the contract within a month's time. She had a prevision of that which was to take place in the near future on the three dimensional plane of life.

The *throne* mentioned in these verses means your authority and your understanding of spiritual and mental laws. You have the authority to mentally and emotionally unite with your good, knowing the creative law of your mind will bring it to pass. You are always at the *throne of God,* for God is Omnipresent, and your separation from His Presence is purely one of thought and belief. The *rainbow round the throne* represents your covenant or agreement with your good; it is symbolic of the seven colors of the solar spectrum which are produced by different rates of vibration of universal energy, which ultimately results in the visible universe. When we go through the seven steps of prayer previously mentioned, the rainbow is round about us because we are reflecting our faith in the God-Presence within in the same manner as water acts as a prism when transmitting the sunlight. The *jasper and sardine stones* represent power and dominion over our thoughts.

The *four and twenty elders* represent all your faculties, feelings, and attitudes gathered together in the contemplation of the Presence and Power of God. Our twelve faculties of mind which look outward must look inward—this represents the disciplining of our faculties of mind which are crowned with gold. *Gold* symbolizes power, and as we learn to discipline our mental faculties we will be able to wield more of God's Power and Wisdom. There are twenty-four hours in the day. Our twelve mental faculties function the twelve hours of the day, and when we are asleep, the same twelve faculties function the twelve hours of night.

(5) *And out of the throne proceeded lightnings and thunderings and voices: and there were seven lamps of fire burning before the throne, which are the seven Spirits of God.*

The *lightnings and thunderings* mean the movement of consciousness from the unconditioned to the conditioned state. In the mental and spiritual creative act we move through the seven qualities or degrees of feeling which are called the *seven Spirits of God.*

(6) *And before the throne there was a sea of glass like unto crystal: and in the midst of the throne, and round about the throne, were four beasts full of eyes before and behind.* (7) *And the first beast was like a lion, and the second beast like a calf, and the third beast had a face as a man, and the fourth beast was like a flying eagle.* (8) *And the four beasts had each of them six wings about him; and they were full of eyes within: and they rest not day and night, saying, Holy, holy, holy, Lord God Almighty, which was, and is, and is to come.*

The *sea of glass* means the mind at peace, in tune with the Infinite. The *four beasts* mean the fourfold constitution of man; they also mean the four horses, the spiritual, mental, emotional, and physical nature of man.

There is another property of the number four that shows us the nature of a solid, thereby revealing to us the story of creation. For under the head of *one* falls what is called in geometry a point; under that of *two* falls a line. If *one* extends itself, *two* is formed; if a point extends itself, a line is formed: a line is length without breadth. If breadth be added, there results a surface, which comes under the category of *three*. To bring a plane to a solid, one thing is needed, depth; and this addition to *three* produces *four*.

There are four stages to producing a solid; the same is true of anything else. We have the seed, the soil, the creative essence, and the plant. In making water in the chemical laboratory we have hydrogen, oxygen, the electric spark, and water. The numeral four may be dramatized in many ways such as the four seasons of the year, four phases of the moon, the four suits in a deck of cards, the four virtues such as prudence, self-mastery, faith, and justice, and the four elements such as fire, water, air, and earth.

The *four beasts* may be explained by the four fixed signs of the Zodiac, Leo, Taurus, Aquarius, and Scorpio. *Leo* represents the lion or the Spiritual Power, and *Taurus* means the calf or bull, the beast of burden. We labor with our desire to make it come true. *Aquarius* (man) signifies the water bearer. *Water* means Truth, which means we meditate on the reality of our desire by pouring water or feeling on our ideal. We imagine the happy ending, remaining loyal and devoted to our ideal. *Scorpio* (eagle) means the impregnation of our subconscious or the finished state. We could explain these four beasts as four phases of consciousness as follows: Consciousness or Spirit, desire, feeling, and realization.

In verse eight the *six wings* refer to the six days of creation, or the length of time it takes you to impregnate the subconscious mind or reach the point of complete mental acceptance. We have to work diligently in all phases of our life to banish negativity and destructive thinking of all kinds. We must watch over our thoughts, ideas, opinions, and reactions, and see to it that nothing crosses the threshold of the mind but that which fills our soul with joy. We must labor mentally in prayer until we reach the Sabbath or seventh day, which is the inner certitude and quiet calm that follows prayer. The *seventh day* or the *Seven Spirits* refer to the six days or six steps leading to the seventh day of rest or conviction. You find the *six* referred to frequently throughout the Bible, such as the six steps to the throne of Solomon and the six pots of water at the marriage feast at Cana. All these references means the same thing, as the Bible uses outer concrete things to portray inner movements of consciousness.

Wings enable you to soar aloft above the storms of life. With your understanding of prayer you can be a spiritual paratrooper and fly over your difficulty to the haven of rest and security—the God-Presence within you. Here you live beyond time and space. In this impregnable fortress no one can lay siege to it. Here you fashion, mold, and direct what is to come, and by conforming your mind to the Truths of God, you bring forth a perfect answer to your prayer.

To say, *"Holy, Holy, Holy,"* is, in our modern parlance, to see the Wholeness, Beauty, and Perfection of God everywhere, in all people, instead of accepting the appearance of discord. *Which was, and is, and is to come* means that the Truths of God change not— they are the same yesterday, today, and forever. You are living in Eternity now, and in the prayer process you do not try to create anything—all you do is identify yourself with that which always was, is now, and ever shall be.

Chapter 5

(1) And I saw in the right hand of him that sat on the throne a book written within and on the backside, sealed with seven seals. (2) And I saw a strong angel proclaiming with a loud voice, Who is worthy to open the book, and to loose the seals thereof? (3) And no man in heaven, nor in earth, neither under the earth, was able to open the book, neither to look thereon. (4) And I wept much, because no man was found worthy to open and to read the book, neither to look thereon.

The *book written within and on the backside* is yourself. Whatever thoughts, beliefs, opinions, theories, or dogmas you write, engrave, or impress on your consciousness, you shall experience them as the objective manifestation of circumstances, conditions, and events. What we write on the inside, we experience on the outside. We have two sides to our life, objective and subjective, visible and invisible, thought and its manifestation.

The *seven seals* are seven states of consciousness. Our concept passes through seven states of awareness wherein we spiritualize our five senses by turning inward to the Spiritual Power; then we get our conscious and subconscious mind to agree and synchronize. When there is no longer any doubt in our conscious or subconscious mind, our prayer is answered. You break the s*even seals* when you discipline your five senses and get the two phases of your mind to agree.

There are *seven seals*. The first is sight; this means to see the Truth about any situation, such as perfect health where sickness is. The second is hearing; you hear the glad tidings by giving your attention to your vision of health. The third is smell; you smell the Truth by coming to a definite decision that the God who made the body can heal it, and you reject all other food, such as false concepts and race belief. The fourth seal is taste; you taste the Truth by appropriating the idea in your mind through meditation and frequent occupancy of the mind regarding the perfect outcome you want; and fifth, you touch the reality of your prayer by feeling the joy of the answered prayer. The remaining two seals, namely your conscious and subconscious mind, means that when you succeed in disciplining the five senses, the male and female principle of your own mind begins to interact harmoniously—a divine marriage takes place between your desire and your emotion, and a child comes forth from the union, which is the answer to your problem.

You are worthy to *open the book* when you give attention to the Creative Principle within you and use it righteously. You will then begin to release the hidden treasures of health, harmony, peace, and beauty in your life.

(5) *And one of the elders saith unto me, Weep not: behold, the Lion of the tribe of Juda, the Root of David, hath prevailed to open the book, and to loose the seven seals thereof.*

The *Lion of the tribe of Juda* can *loose the seven seals*—the lion is the king of the jungle. Man is also a king when he awakens to the Power of God within him; he can take charge of his conceptive realm, regulate his emotions and reactions, and refuse to give a passport to any negative thought wishing to enter his mind. He can issue decrees and orders which must be obeyed implicitly, because he knows whatever he decrees with faith and confidence, his subconscious mind will validate, honor, and bring forth into his objective experience. Man's power to think, imagine, and feel constructively gives him power over all conditions in his world; he can *open the seals* which have been covered up and sealed by ignorance, fear, and superstition.

(6) *And I beheld, and, lo, in the midst of the throne and of the four beasts, and in the midst of the elders, stood a Lamb as it had been slain, having seven horns and seven eyes, which are the seven Spirits of God sent forth into all the earth.*

The *Lamb* is an ancient symbol of the first sign of the zodiac. The Zodiac means your consciousness or infinity, where all tones, moods, feelings, and vibrations are. You can strike any tone, because man is the infinite keyboard of God. What tone do you strike? I suggest you play the melody of God by striking the tones of wisdom, truth, and beauty; of harmony, health, and peace; of joy, wholeness, and perfection. The *Lamb* means your Consciousness which is forever dying to the old and being resurrected to new convictions of health, wealth, etc. If sick, you can detach yourself from the sick state and mentally feast on the Truth that God is Absolute Harmony and Absolute Perfection, and as you do, the old state dies and the new state of consciousness is born.

When the sun crossed the equator on the twenty-first of March, which is called the ingress of Aries, the ancients said, "This is the Lamb of God that taketh away the sins of the world," for the simple reason that as the sun crosses the equator in spring, all the seeds frozen in the ground during the long winter months are resurrected, and the desert rejoices once more and blossoms as the rose. All nature rejoices as the glow, warmth, and radiance of the sunlight redeems the world from the darkness of winter to the joy and enthusiasm of spring. It was called the *Lamb* because the sun entered the sign of the ram or lamb; symbolically this means your mind or intellect which is illumined by the Light or Wisdom of God.

You possess this Wisdom when you know that the Almighty Power of God flows through your mental patterns and mental imagery; therefore you will begin to reproduce the qualities, attributes, and potencies of God through your constructive patterns of thought. Man creates the same way God creates. God imagines Himself to be something; then He becomes what he imagines Himself to be.

The *seven horns* and the *seven eyes* are the seven powers and seven perceptions about which we have elaborated in this chapter.

(8) *And when he had taken the book, the four beasts and four and twenty elders fell down before the Lamb, having every one of them harps, and golden vials full of odours, which are the prayers of saints.*

The *golden vials full of odours* represent the fragrant state, the reaction which satisfies. You cannot suppress the joy which arises when you succeed in feeling the reality of what you prayed for. You have a harp because prayer is the music of the soul. As you walk the earth the Light of God goes before you, behind you, to the right and left of you, above and below you—these are also the *six wings* or the six ways God surrounds you. The four powers are with you, and each of them has six wings.

(11) *And I beheld, and I heard the voice of many angels round about the throne and the beasts and the elders: and the number of them was ten thousand times ten thousand, and thousands of thousands.*

The *tens of thousands* mentioned represent the hundreds of thousands of thoughts in your mind; not all of them are constructive. For example you might say, "I fear, I can't, I'm weak, I resent," *etc.* Which I is speaking? It is not the Infinite in you, or the real I. All these thoughts must die, and you must begin to think, speak, and act from the standpoint of the Infinite Goodness of God, the Infinite Intelligence of God, the Boundless Love of God, and the Omnipotence of the Infinite One. As you do this you will begin to hear the *voice of the angels*. An *angel* is a messenger of God or the Truth of God operating in your mind. The many angels operating in your mind are faith, confidence, love, joy, good will, enthusiasm, and understanding.

Angels are attitudes of mind or states of consciousness. An angel is also an idea or desire which you have. Give your attention to the angel, mentally and emotionally identify with it, and it shall come to pass through the creative law of your mind.

Chapter 6

(1) And I saw when the Lamb opened one of the seals, and I heard, as it were the noise of thunder, one of the four beasts saying, Come and see. (2) And I saw, and behold a white horse: and he that sat on him had a bow; and a crown was given unto him: and he went forth conquering, and to conquer. (3) And when he had opened the second seal, I heard the second beast say, Come and see. (4) And there went out another horse that was red: and power was given to him that sat thereon to take peace from the earth, and that they should kill one another: and there was given unto him a great sword.

The *Four Horsemen of the Apocalypse* are really the four beasts we have been talking about, and the four beasts in action in us become the four horses. We become aware of the functioning of our mind through understanding the meaning of these picturesque symbols. We must not construe as history anything in the *Book of Revelation*, as it is purely allegorical and mystical. This is why it is unintelligible to the average person, because its subject-matter is veiled in symbolical language. In ancient times secrecy was always maintained regarding the sacred science for the sole purpose of guarding it and preserving it from dictators, despots, and tyrants, as well as from those who were considered unworthy to receive it.

The *Four Horsemen* represent the four elements of our nature, such as the spiritual, intellectual, emotional, and physical aspects of our being. The *white horse* symbolizes the Divine Presence in you, God, I AM, and the Higher Self, your spiritual nature. You ride the *white horse* when you realize that your own Consciousness or Awareness is the only Cause, Substance, and Power. When you trust the God-Presence completely, when you give all your allegiance and devotion to the sovereignty and supremacy of the One Power, you are truly riding the *white horse.*

The *bow* mentioned refers to the bow and arrow which is a symbol for the word which you send forth. The *word* means your inner thought and feeling which you send forth. In other words if you have an idea, this is the arrow which you are aiming for the bull's eye. If you hit your target, well and good. Our prayers are answered the way we believe; therefore all prayers are answered at the level of our consciousness. The word spoken audibly or silently does not return to us void, based on the fact that it is done unto us as we believe. When you *ride the white horse*, you wear a *crown* which symbolizes victory, accomplishment, and achievement. When you assume that the Almighty Power is moving on your behalf, you will always be the victor. There is no power to challenge God or Spirit which always moves as a unity. When you pray or think, realize it is Omnipotence thinking in you, and there is nothing to challenge the One Power. Do this and wonders will happen as you pray.

The Eastern scriptures refer to the *white horse* as follows: "Prajapati said, 'Whoever shall seek thee (God) in the form of a white horse shall find thee.'" In ancient Vedic lore, the Sun was referred to as the zodiacal horse which died to save all flesh. This is another form of the great solar allegory common to all religions of the world. The birth, death, and resurrection of the Sun represent the mind awakening to the Indwelling God; then the death of ignorance, fear, and lack, and the resurrection of the qualities and potencies of God takes place. This is what religion is all about.

The *red horse* symbolizes the mind energized by a strong and wonderful desire to be, to do, and to have. Desire is the root of every conceivable mode of life.

Desire is the mainspring of all action; it is the cause of all feeling and action. When you desire, you wish to bring forth something which exists only in your thought. Desire is behind all progress; it is the force behind all things. Desire indicates a preference for one thing over another; it implies selection. Desire is the Voice of God in you, telling you to rise higher. Desire and fulfillment are bound together as cause and effect. When we have a desire, there is warfare in our mind because we are in a divided state. The *sword* of the Spirit signifies the awareness of Spiritual Power which dissipates all negation in the mind and brings peace.

Doubt, fear, race beliefs, evidence of senses, verdicts of the world, and circumstances challenge you in your mind. You must use the sword of Truth by realizing that you can overcome all the problems by what you know. Your confidence and faith come from awareness of the Spiritual Power and its responsiveness to you and to whatever you claim, believing you will receive. You *ride the red horse* when you know that the God who gave you the desire is the same God who fulfills it, and it is easy for the Father Indwelling to bring it to pass. You are now armed with the sword of Truth which chops the head off the negative thoughts, enabling you to lift up your ideal to the point of acceptance. The old state is dead—behold, the new!

(5) *And when he had opened the third seal, I heard the third beast say, Come and see. And I beheld, and lo a black horse; and he that sat on him had a pair of balances in his hand.* (6) *And I heard a voice in the midst of the four beasts say, A measure of wheat for a penny, and three measures of barley for a penny; and see thou hurt not the oil and the wine.*

One of the meanings of a *black horse* is false knowledge and illusion is the rider. But now you are definitely and positively coming to a decision or a state of balance and equilibrium in your mind. The *wheat* and *barley* are bread substance signifying the food of the world or race mind beliefs. We weigh this with a small measure by giving fear, doubt, and race beliefs no power at all; then the limitation or problem is wasting away as we fast from fear and false beliefs and feast on faith and trust in the One Power Which does all things. We weigh all things by reasoning things out spiritually, knowing in our heart that fear, doubt, and worry have no power, no principle behind them, nothing to sustain them, and that they are a conglomeration of sinister shadows in the mind, an illusion of power.

You ride the third horse when you look at your desire and weigh it with the mood of receptivity by saying decisively and incisively to yourself, "This I am going to accept. I am going to imagine, feel, and continue to hear the good news of the possibility of the execution of my desire, and I will bring it to pass." You have tipped the scales in favor of your desire, and there is no argument in your mind. You ride the black horse as a master horseman when you listen to the good news rather than to limitation and negation. We do not *waste the oil and the wine*, which is an exhortation to protect the growth of love (*oil*) for God and the Good, and wisdom (*wine*) which is an awareness of the Presence and Power of God and how to release the hidden treasures.

(7) *And when he had opened the fourth seal, I heard the voice of the fourth beast say, Come and see. (8) And I looked, and behold a pale horse: and his name that sat on him was Death, and Hell followed with him. And power was given unto them over the fourth part of the earth, to kill with sword, and with hunger, and with death, and with the beasts of the earth.*

The pale horse means death, *i.e.,* the death of the old state and the birth of the new. When something dies, something is born. Every end is a beginning. Before something is created, something must be destroyed. You must ride with the idea or desire in your mind until you no longer desire it. The desire is now dead, just as a seed undergoes dissolution in the soil bequeathing or releasing its energy to another form of itself. Your desire has pierced the deeper layers of the subconscious mind, and the new state will now come forth. You must die to your present limitation before you can live to that which you long to be. The *Hell* mentioned in verse eight means Hades or the subjective self where the old state is consumed and the new is born. Through prayer you change the subconscious mind; then the ulcerous or the cancerous condition disappears. Whatever the problem or difficulty may be, it is due to a negative pattern in the subconscious mind, and when we change the subconscious, the objective manifestation must disappear.

The *fourth part* mentioned means your body, environment, conditions, and circumstances. Whatever troubles you may have in any phase of your life can be transformed with the sword of Truth, by fasting mentally from the problem and feasting on the solution; then dissolution or death of the old will take place, and the Infinite One makes all things new.

(9) *And when he had opened the fifth seal, I saw under the altar the souls of them that were slain for the word of God, and for the testimony which they beheld: (10) And they cried with a loud voice, saying, How long, O Lord, holy and true, dost thou not judge and avenge our blood on them that dwell on the earth?*

In the outside world vengeance means *to get even* with someone who has wronged you; then the wrong-

doer will again take vengeance and will try *to get even*.
Thus it becomes a vicious circle which never ends.
In the Bible *vengeance* means balance, equilibrium,
or vindication of the Truth. *Vengeance is mine; I will
repay, saith the Lord* (Rom. 12:19.) The Lord is our consciousness; vengeance takes place in consciousness
when we cast out the envy, jealousy, and other negative states (*I saw under the altar the souls of them that
were slain*) and replace them with spiritual values—
the eternal verities. We rise in consciousness through
contemplation of God, we get even, *i.e.,* we get equilibrium, we enter into peace.

If someone has hurt you, realize that you, through
your own thinking process, have hurt yourself, you
have permitted your own thoughts and emotions to
run wild. If you are now angry with some person, pray
as follows: "The Harmony, Peace, and Love of God
flowing through me now are also flowing through the
other person." Continue to do this frequently, and
you will find all the roots of ill will and hostility in
your subconscious will wither away, and you are free.
You have vindicated the Truth, and the Truth sets you
free. This is vengeance when properly understood.

(12) *And I beheld when he had opened the sixth
seal, and lo, there was a great earthquake; and the sun
became black as sackcloth of hair, and the moon became
as blood; (13) And the stars of heaven fell unto the earth,*

even as a fig tree casteth her untimely figs, when she is shaken of a mighty wind.

Six is the number of creation, and when your prayer is answered there is always an earthquake because there is a dissolution of the old state before the new comes forth. The darkest hour is before the dawn. The sun and the moon are ancient symbols for the conscious and subconscious mind. When a woman gives birth, blood and water come out. She forgets the pangs and pains of childbirth and gets lost in the joy of beholding the newborn child. All this is symbolic of the birth of a new awareness in ourselves. *The sackcloth of hair* mentioned in verse twelve means disciplining of your thoughts by turning away from the allurements of sense evidence and placing all your reliance in the Divine. *Thou has turned for me my mourning into dancing: thou hast put off my sackcloth, and girded me with gladness.* (Ps. 30:11.)

The fig tree is a symbol of the sweet fruit of the Tree of Life. *The fruit of the Spirit is love, joy, peace, longsuffering, gentleness, goodness, faith, meekness, temperance: against such there is no law.* (GAL. 5:22, 23.) When the figs fall off the fig tree (*as a fig tree casteth her untimely figs*), those that remain are the best. The same takes place in our own mind, we fertilize and give attention only to those concepts and ideas which strengthen, heal, bless, and inspire us; we select our supreme desire, we subjectify it, plant it, keep our attention upon it; then we rest until creation takes place.

(14) *And the heaven departed as a scroll when it is rolled together; and every mountain and island were moved out of their places.*

Our old states disintegrate and fade away. The mountains and islands represent the obstacles, fixed false beliefs and difficulties which vanish in the presence of the Truth which frees.

(17) *For the great day of his wrath is come; and who shall be able to stand?*

The wrath of God is the action of the Spiritual Power in your mind, body, and environment. Sometimes there is a crisis in illness and the patient seems to get worse before he gets better. The Healing Presence is at work destroying all the bacteria or virulent organisms and suddenly the temperature drops, the patient smiles, and a healing follows. The cleansing process of the mind and body is called the wrath of God. The wrath of God does not mean the fury of an angry God; on the contrary it means the activity of the Divine Power bringing order out of chaos and restoring your life and affairs according to the Divine Pattern which is order, harmony, and peace. The wrath of God could be likened to spring cleaning that takes place when everything in the house is disarranged and dirt is everywhere; only when you finish and put everything in its proper place, will you see Divine Order everywhere. The day of God's wrath in your life is something supremely worth experiencing, for it means God in action in your life, resulting in harmony, health, peace, and abundance.

Chapter 7

(1) And after these things I saw four angels standing on the four corners of the earth, holding the four winds of the earth, that the wind should not blow on the earth, nor on the sea, nor on any tree. (2) And I saw another angel ascending from the east, having the seal of the living God: and he cried with a loud voice to the four angels, to whom it was given to hurt the earth and the sea.

The *four angels* are within you which means your acquaintance with your fourfold nature. The first angel is your awareness that the Spirit within you is God, the Supreme Power. The second angel is your desire, the realization of which would free you from any predicament. The third angel is your feeling, conviction or complete mental absorption of your desire. The fourth angel is the manifestation or objectification of your desire. Your knowledge of the Creative Law and its fourfold function enables you to choose from the treasure house of Infinity all those things that would bless and prosper you. The *winds* referred to are the moods or feelings which are impressed on the subjective mind and which come forth into objective experience as form, function, conditions and events.

An angel is an attitude of mind, a way of thinking; it is the angel that always announces the birth of our savior. A knowledge of the workings of your subconscious mind is an angel because such knowledge enables you to liberate yourself from any difficulty. An angel is like the morning star which heralds the coming of the sun that redeems the earth from darkness and causes the whole heavens to become a blaze of glory. Your mood of confidence and faith in God is an angel that goes before you making straight, joyous, and happy your way. The sun rises in the east to open and govern the day; symbolically the angel ascending from the east is your awareness of the I AM within you as God. Your I AMness is Lord God Almighty—the only Cause, Substance, and Power in the world. Your consciousness of God directs all the other angels (thoughts, ideas, desires) within you. Your spiritual awareness directs and orders all your thoughts, feelings, and emotions. You are in command and you order your thoughts around in the same manner as an employer tells his employees what to do. The *loud voice* mentioned in verse two is your dominant conviction in the Infinite Goodness of God, and living in the joyous expectancy of the best. You are the man of authority ordering your servants (thoughts, ideas, and concepts) to give attention to things divine.

(3) *Saying, Hurt not the earth, neither the sea, nor the trees, till we have sealed the servants of our God in their foreheads. (4) And I heard the number of them which were sealed: and there were sealed an hundred and forty and four thousand of all the tribes of the children of Israel.*

The earth is your body and environment, your objective world; *the sea* represents your emotion; *the trees* are ideas and thoughts which have grown up into fixed attitudes and convictions; and when you *seal* the servants of God in your forehead, you are consciously and subconsciously convinced of the truths which you affirm, and nothing can hurt you as you give no power to the world or external phenomena. Your *forehead* represents your conscious mind, and when the subjective wisdom of God anoints your intellect, you have sealed the servants of God in your intellect. Your thoughts from now on will be noble and Godlike, and true feeling follows your true thoughts. Verse four refers to our twelve faculties of mind. Consciousness multiplies and magnifies everything it touches.

Your twelve powers, when disciplined, are magnified exceedingly and are called the one hundred forty-four thousand. When you awaken your faculties, they become powerful.

(9) *After this I beheld, and, lo, a great multitude, which no man could number, of all nations, and kindreds, and people, and tongues, stood before the throne, and before the Lamb, clothed with white robes, and palms in their hands.*

All men in the world are extensions of yourself. You are the multitude and the two and a half billion people in this world are projections of yourself. When the bell tolls for anyone in the world, it tolls for you also. There is but One Man and we are all manifestations of the One Man and the One Life. Man would not recognize the cells of his own body when seen under the microscope, neither would he recognize the hair of his own head or drops of blood from his own veins. In like manner, the unawakened, unillumined man does not recognize other men as parts of himself. When we begin to discipline our twelve faculties through prayer and meditation, we receive the palms of victory and triumph.

(14) *And I said unto him, Sir, thou knowest. And he said to me, These are they which came out of great tribulation, and have washed their robes, and made them white in the blood of the Lamb.*

We *wash our robes* when we discipline our mental faculties, attitudes, and feelings. In other words, we dress mentally for God, and when we come into His Presence we wear the robes as moods of love, joy, and expectancy. We cannot come to the banquet table of God wearing the robes or garments of fear, anger, jealousy, resentment, prejudice, or condemnation. We cleanse ourselves by pouring out love on others, by wishing health, happiness, peace, and good will for them. Love is the fulfilling of the law of health, abundance, and security. *White* symbolizes purity and sincerity. *The blood of the Lamb* means the Life and Love of God. As we enter into the consciousness of God's Love, everything unlike God in our mind or heart is dissolved. *Blood* means Life, and Life is Love, and God is Love. When you give life, love, and attention to the ideas which elevate, bless, and heal you, you are saved by the blood of the Lamb.

The Lamb is a world symbol of sacrifice referring to the sacrifice or the giving up of our negative thoughts, emotions, and destructive passions for the purpose of making a place in our soul for the qualities of goodness, truth, and love. We give up the lesser for the greater. We sacrifice a lower way of life in order to cultivate and enjoy a higher life. All progress is a sacrifice in this sense. The sacrifices and burnt offerings in general signify the regeneration and spiritual unfoldment of man by wisdom, truth, beauty, and love. In simple language, the *Lamb of God* is the desire of your heart, for desire is the gift of God, and you must sacrifice or offer up your desire through feeling its reality so that it dies in your subconscious, and is resurrected as answered prayer.

(15) *Therefore are they before the throne of God, and serve him day and night in his temple: and he that sitteth on the throne shall dwell among them.*

The spiritually minded man sits on the throne of his own consciousness maintaining control of his own twelve faculties, and he judges everything according to spiritual standards and the Truth of God.

Chapter 8

(1) And when he had opened the seventh seal, there was silence in heaven about the space of half an hour. (2) And I saw the seven angels which stood before God; and to them were given seven trumpets.

The *seventh seal* is the same as the seventh day or the seventh tone which means the stillness, the rest, the silence which follows true prayer. *Half an hour* means half time which is an indefinite term for we know nothing of the mystery of creation. The ways of our subconscious are past finding out. We do not know how, where, or through what source the answer comes. It comes in ways we know not of, in a manner which we know not, and in an hour when we expect it not. We sow an idea in the subconscious by meditating on it; there it gestates in the darkness, and when the time is ripe, the subjective wisdom brings it to pass according to its own way.

(3) *And another angel came and stood at the altar, having a golden censer; and there was given unto him much incense, that he should offer it with the prayers of all saints upon the golden altar which was before the throne.*

The seven angels of the seven churches are seven degrees of awareness. We discipline these seven degrees of awareness (seven states of consciousness). Then we blow the seven trumpets, the trumpets sound the call to action. This means that out of our silent meditation there issues a mood, feeling, and confidence in the law, knowing that a response is coming forth. All this is accomplished without strain or effort, just a silent inner knowing of the soul.

(4) *And the smoke of the incense, which came with the prayers of the saints, ascended up before God out of the angel's hand.*

This means that our consciousness is at the place where the prospect seems so beautiful, so fragrant, that all our senses are turned inward toward our good. Our good has become alive in our heart; we see and hear on the inside—this is incense.

(7) *The first angel sounded, and there followed hail and fire mingled with blood, and they were cast upon the earth: and the third part of trees was burnt up, and all green grass was burnt up. (8) And the second angel sounded, and as it were a great mountain burning with*

fire was cast into the sea: and the third part of the sea became blood; (9) And the third part of the creatures which were in the sea, and had life, died; and the third part of the ships were destroyed. (10) And the third angel sounded, and there fell a great star from heaven, burning as it were a lamp, and it fell upon the third part of the rivers, and upon the fountains of waters; (11) And the name of the star is called Wormwood: and the third part of the waters became wormwood; and many men died of the waters, because they were made bitter. (12) And the fourth angel sounded, and the third part of the sun was smitten, and the third part of the moon, and the third part of the stars; so as the third part of them was darkened, and the day shone not for a third part of it, and the night likewise. (13) And I beheld, and heard an angel flying through the midst of heaven, saying with a loud voice, Woe, woe, woe, to the inhabiters of the earth by reason of the other voices of the trumpet of the three angels, which are yet to sound!

Here we have a story of changing from the old state to the new. Our moods, thoughts, and limitations are burned up by the fire of Divine Love and constructive thinking. *A tree* represents fixed opinions and beliefs which grow up in our mind. *A ship* represents emotions and feelings. *The third part* represents the trinity, or the mental and spiritual creative acts which enable us to destroy all negative patterns in the subconscious mind. *The trinity* is mind, idea, and expression, or thinker, thought, and action. The Divine Trinity is known as Father, Son, and Holy Spirit which means consciousness, idea, and feeling. *The fourth part* is the objective manifestation of what we feel as true. In verse nine when it says, "The sea became blood," *blood* means Life, and when we are very negative and depressed, we tend to resist the influx of the Spiritual Power. The waters of *life are bitter* meaning our mind and emotions are full of bitterness, ill will, and hostility as long as we are separated from God and His Peace. Prayer or the practice of the Presence of God will dissolve all these states, and we will be healed.

Chapter 9

(1) *And the fifth angel sounded, and I saw a star fall from heaven unto the earth: and to him was given the key of the bottomless pit. (2) And he opened the bottomless pit; and there arose a smoke out of the pit, as the smoke of a great furnace; and the sun and the air were darkened by reason of the smoke of the pit. (3) And there came out of the smoke locusts upon the earth: and unto them was given power, as the scorpions of the earth have power. (4) And it was commanded them that they should not hurt the grass of the earth, neither any green thing, neither any tree; but only those men which have not the seal of God in their foreheads.*

The *star that falls from heaven* means Lucifer (Light Bearer) or Satan. *And he said unto them, I beheld Satan as lightning fall from heaven.* (Lu. 10:18.) *How art thou fallen from heaven, O Lucifer.* (Isa. 14:12.)

Lucifer or Satan can, in one sense, be compared to Judas. Judas betrays (which means reveals) Jesus, then commits suicide; so when Judas or our sense of lack or limitation dies, this gives rise to our savior or saving state of consciousness. When a man dies to the belief in poverty, he is born to the idea of wealth; when a man dies to hatred, he gives birth to love; when he dies to anger, he gives birth to harmony and good will. Lucifer could also be likened to Venus. Venus, the morning star, heralds or reveals the birth of the sun; likewise our problem reveals our savior. If in prison, you want freedom; if sick, you want health; if thirsty, you want water. Water would be your savior if you were dying of thirst in the desert. Lucifer, like Judas, is our sense of lack which must die before the savior can come in. We cannot have our savior, the state that will bless us, before the sense of lack drops from consciousness. When Lucifer (sense of lack) falls from heaven (consciousness), he heralds our savior. Our savior is the realization of our heart's desire.

Verses one and two refer to the subjective mind which is the place of death or dissolution of negative states, complexes, fears, *etc.*; also it is the law of life. The seed we deposit in the soil undergoes dissolution at the same time bequeathing its energy, vitality, and force to another form of itself. The seed must first die to give life to something new. Our desire must die in the subconscious which takes place whenever we succeed through feeling in impregnating our subconscious mind; then comes forth the manifestation or answer to our prayer.

The seal of God in the forehead means your conviction in the supremacy of the Spiritual Power. The *forehead* means your intellect or conscious mind which is aware of spiritual values. The *seal of God* is on our foreheads when you know that the law of God responds immediately to your positive thought. We have a new name or nature because our assurance, our confidence and our faith are capable of granting life to more and more Godlike qualities in our life. The locusts represent the food of the five senses which disturb and frighten us, but when we know that the external world has no power over us and that Spirit alone is the cause, we are free, and the locusts or fears of the world fail to move us.

(13) *And the sixth angel sounded, and I heard a voice from the four horns of the golden altar which is before God,* (14) *Saying to the sixth angel which had the trumpet, Loose the four angels which are bound in the great river Euphrates.*

The *four horns* are symbols of your consciousness and its four powers which have been covered previously, such as Father (consciousness), Son (idea, desire), Holy Ghost (feeling of wholeness or oneness with your desire, and the fourth part—objectification of your desire, or the son made manifest). Verse fourteen is the same as the previous verse indicating a propelling movement as consciousness. *Euphrates* means the Creative Power within you whereby you fructify and bring forth the glory of God.

(15) *And the number of the army of the horsemen were two hundred thousand thousand: and I heard the number of them. (17) And thus I saw the horses in the vision, and them that sat on them, having breastplates of fire, and of jacinth, and brimstone: and the heads of the horses were as the heads of lions; and out of their mouths issued fire and smoke and brimstone.*

The vast armies of horsemen represent the limitless power of the God-Presence. The *men killed by fire* represent thoughts, opinions, beliefs which are dissolved by fire or Divine Intelligence and understanding of the truths of God and Life. The spiritual concepts or the armies of heaven destroy the evil, false, superstitious thoughts, and negative tendencies of man.

Chapter 10

(1) *And I saw another mighty angel come down from heaven, clothed with a cloud: and a rainbow was upon his head, and his face was as it were the sun, and his feet as pillars of fire: (2) And he had in his hand a little book open: and he set his right foot upon the sea, and his left foot on the earth, (3) And cried with a loud voice, as when a lion roareth: and when he had cried, seven thunders uttered their voices. (4) And when the seven thunders had uttered their voices, I was about to write: and I heard a voice from heaven saying unto me, Seal up those things which the seven thunders uttered, and write them not.*

The *little book* is the subjective mind, where we write, engrave all the concepts, all our impressions and beliefs. *The right foot on the sea* means to discipline the mind by the right understanding of the law. We are all living in the sea of mind and emotions, and we must learn that the pathway of love is open to everyone in all circumstances, and upon which you may step this moment. You need no special training to place your right foot on the sea. Feet mean understanding in Bible language. You can begin this moment steadfastly to expel from your mentality every thought of ill will, bitterness, or personal condemnation, of resentment, and of anything and everything which is contrary to the Golden Rule and the Law of Love. Fall in love with the eternal verities, love, goodness, truth, good will, honesty, and justice. Love will heal you; love will comfort you and bless you in countless ways. Love will illumine your pathway and give you peace of mind.

You place your left foot on the earth in this sense. *Earth* means manifestation such as your body, environment, conditions, *etc.* The *left foot* means that you know that the subjective condition will always overturn and overthrow the objective condition. You can always go within and visualize the way you want things to be, and the silent inner movement of consciousness will bring about outer conditions to conform to your inner conviction. All doubt and fear drop away as we become aware of our Hidden Power. *The seven thunders* are seven qualities of consciousness. *The mighty angel* spoken of is your unwavering, unshakable conviction which comes from the heavens of your own illumined mind. *Seven* means completion which symbolizes the lion, the conquering state of consciousness.

Verse four means we must rest in the conviction that our prayer is answered. The adversary or negative thought may come into our mind to challenge us and disturb us. We must not listen to anything but that which we know to be true. We must feel our new concept, clinch it, and wait in faith, believing until manifestation takes place.

(9) *And I went unto the angel, and said unto him, Give me the little book. And he said unto me, Take it, and eat it up; and it shall make thy belly bitter, but it shall be in thy mouth sweet as honey.*

When we first hear the truth that the Creative Power responds to every thought, we become very enthusiastic and it seems sweet and fragrant. However, at times our senses become overwhelmed by what we see and hear, and we lose the true perception of the One Power. When we admit another power, we begin to oppose and resist it. Our desire or ideal at such times is like food which we have not properly digested (*it shall make thy belly bitter, but in thy mouth sweet as honey*). When you contemplate your desire, you generate a new mood, but if you think there is something blocking you, or some external agency that can thwart you, then you are in the peculiar and difficult position of fighting and quarreling with your own thought. This creates confusion, irritability, and anger; this is a quarrel of your mind which resembles the quarrel in the stomach when the food is not properly digested and assimilated. If you believe in a power of evil, you are actually denying the power of the One God and His Omnipotence. This creates a conflict and we do not succeed in digesting, absorbing, and assimilating our desire or consciousness. The answer to the whole question is that you have to identify yourself with the Universal Power from whence your strength, power, and faith comes. Remember that you are a child of God, and all the powers of God are locked within you in the same way that the palm tree is locked within the seed. Become receptive now and say, "I accept my good, God gave it to me, and I allow it to take form in my experience."

(11) *And he said unto me, Thou must prophesy again before many peoples, and nations, and tongues, and kings.*

We must always *prophesy* by feeling and knowing that the Infinite Goodness of God is forever flowing through us and that we are channels of the Divine. Our mood, feeling, the animation in the inside determines our future. We must become the true prophet and prophesy or claim only that which is true of God in our lives. According to our faith in God is it done unto us.

Chapter 11

(1) And there was given me a reed like unto a rod: and the angel stood, saying, Rise, and measure the temple of God, and the altar, and them that worship therein. (2) But the court which is without the temple leave out, and measure it not; for it is given unto the Gentiles: and the holy city shall they tread under foot forty and two months. (3) And I will give power unto my two witnesses, and they shall prophesy a thousand two hundred and threescore days, clothed in sackcloth.

A rod is a symbol of authority actively exercised. Consciousness is the only authority. We can have nothing except by rights of consciousness. Man is the measurer. *We measure the temple of God* by our degree of faith, awareness, or inner conviction of God's infinite goodness, and according to our measure or degree of acceptance and receptivity is it done unto us.

In verse two, the *outer court* is the world of appearances. We do not measure the outer court because we work on the inside realm of the mind; and what we feel and accept as true on the inside we shall experience on the outside. *Forty and two months* indicate an indefinite time. It means three and a half years literally. The number four in Bible symbolism means objectification or manifestation, the completed cycle. In other words, the manner in which our prayer will be answered is hidden from us, and we know not the day, hour, or minute in which the answer comes with healing on its wings. Our negative thoughts, fears, opinions, and beliefs must be redeemed with the Light of God, otherwise they will tread underfoot, or keep from perfect expression and demonstration, the spirituality or God consciousness within man.

(4) *These are the two olive trees, and the two candlesticks standing before the God of the earth.* (5) *And if any man will hurt them, fire proceedeth out of their mouth, and devoureth their enemies: and if any man will hurt them, he must in this manner be killed.* (6) *These have power to shut heaven, that it rain not in the days of their prophecy: and have power over waters to turn them to blood, and to smite the earth with all plagues, as often as they will.* (7) *And when they shall have finished their testimony, the beast that ascendeth out of the bottomless pit shall make war against them, and shall overcome*

them, and kill them. (8) And their dead bodies shall lie in the street of the great city, which spiritually is called Sodom and Egypt, where also our Lord was crucified.

These verses deal with the story of the two witnesses which are Love and Wisdom. *Love* is loyalty and adherence to the One Power, and *Wisdom* represents the true idea. These two testify to a third to come. The son or answer to our prayer will come when our I AM marries or unites itself with our ideal. The *two witnesses* or *two olive trees* represent the way by which the oil or nature of God or Spirit is brought into manifestation in our lives. The union of two things brings forth a third. The union of a father and mother brings forth a child. Your true idea enveloped in love will come forth as form, function, experience, condition, or event.

The beast that cometh up out of the abyss represents a dominant race thought which browbeats you, preventing the two witnesses within you from functioning so that they remain seemingly inactive. However, Truth always wins, error has no principle behind it and nothing to back it up, and as you continue to affirm the truths of God in faith and love, the error, the adversary, will be cast out of heaven (your mind in tune with the Infinite).

The city of *Sodom* and the *dead bodies* mentioned in verses eight and nine mean the world of the five senses where the tyranny of false beliefs and negative passions reign supreme. When our consciousness is undisciplined, it is like a Sodomite, a harlot; it will join with anything, *i.e.,* cohabit with envy, jealousy, hate, revenge, greed, lust, *etc.* In verse eight, it says our Lord was crucified in Sodom and Egypt. Your Lord is the dominant idea in your mind, that which you give most attention to. If you desire a healing, you take your attention away from your body, its aches and pains, and focus all your attention on the idea of health and harmony. As you continue to do this with faith and understanding, it becomes a dominant force in your life, and this idea is impregnated in Egypt or your subconscious mind where it gestates in the darkness. It is said to die in the subconscious mind, and after a while it is resurrected as perfect health for you. Your Lord or dominant idea crossed over from your conscious mind to your subconscious mind. Furthermore, as you filled your mind with the truth of the Healing Power of God's Love, you crowded out of the mind everything unlike God or the good. The dead bodies mentioned in verses eight and nine represent the destruction and the negative thoughts in your mind.

(15) *And the seventh angel sounded; and there were great voices in heaven, saying, The kingdoms of this world are become the kingdoms of our Lord, and of his Christ; and he shall reign for ever and ever.*

The *seventh angel* represents fulfillment, conviction, the inner sound or movement of the heart which tells us that all is well, that we rest in God.

(19) *And the temple of God was opened in heaven, and there was seen in his temple the ark of his testament: and there were lightnings, and voices, and thunderings, and an earthquake, and great hail.*

You build your *ark* on the understanding of the wisdom, presence, and power of God. The *ark* is built by claiming what is true of God is true of you. You can build this ark in the midst of all the errors and false beliefs of the mind. As you continue in your mental and spiritual practices, an earthquake will take place in the sense that everything unlike God or the truth will be destroyed in your life; it will seem like an earthquake because the old man will be destroyed and a new man will appear transformed by faith and love of God. Your ark is your covenant or agreement with the GodSelf within you that you shall inherit all that the Father has. *All things that the Father hath are mine.* (John 16:15.) The destruction, annihilation, and consuming of all your race thoughts and erroneous concepts through the fire of Divine Love is really the earthquake that destroys the old and gives birth to the new.

Behold, I make all things new. (Rev. 21:5.)

Chapter 12

(1) And there appeared a great wonder in heaven; a woman clothed with the sun, and the moon under her feet, and upon her head a crown of twelve stars. And she being with child cries travailing in birth, and pained to be delivered. And there appeared another wonder in heaven; and behold a great red dragon, having seven heads and ten horns, and seven crowns upon his heads. (4) And his tail drew the third part of the stars of heaven, and did cast them to the earth: and the dragon stood before the woman which was ready to be delivered, for to devour her child as soon as it was born.

T he *sun and moon* represent the conscious and subconscious minds. The *crown of twelve stars* on her head indicates the illumined, disciplined conscious mind which entertains only the noble, Godlike con-

cepts. When there is agreement between the conscious and subconscious minds, our prayers are always
answered and countless blessings follow.

*If two of you shall agree . . . as touching any thing
that they shall ask, it shall be done for them of my
Father which is in heaven.* (Matt. 18:19.) This is a
simple statement of the law of your own mind, indicating that when you unite yourself mentally and
emotionally with your desire, the subjective mind
validates and brings what you request to pass. You
are the woman clothed with the sun when you are
mentally married to your highest ideal. The *dragon*
is Satan, the *adversary*, the negative force. Our
thoughts come in pairs. Every good and wonderful
idea you have may be challenged instantaneously
by some negative and ignoble thought, its opposite.
Have you not noticed that when you affirm perfect
health for your friend, the thought comes to you,
"He cannot be healed," "He is incurable," *etc.* The
dragon which stands before the woman about to be
delivered is negation, the race mind, lack of understanding, and false beliefs, all of which tend to tempt
you away from your faith in your good. *Though he
slay me, yet will I trust him.* You can always rise in
your mind over any obstacle, challenge, temptation,
race pattern, and over all objective evidence. Have
confidence in the One Creative Power and this atti-

tude will enable you to think above all the suggested patterns of the race mind, and you will succeed in bringing to pass the cherished desires of your heart. If you allow the false, erroneous concept of the world to rule in your mind, you will slay the child or the new awareness of God in your mind.

The Indwelling Power or Spiritual Idea is spoken of in the Bible as a child. The subconscious mind is the woman spoken of in the Bible, and your awareness of the Presence, Power and Intelligence of God locked in your subconscious depths is described as a child. When your conscious mind discovers that the Indwelling God is the Spirit in all of us, the very Life of us, we begin to use this Power; this is called the birth of the child. The old habit pattern of thought, the theological God living in the skies, an anthropomorphic being who punishes and tests us, all these concepts come to our mind to challenge our new concept. We must constantly remind ourselves of this Indwelling Power, nourish and guard our faith in this God-Presence; and as we do this the child, or our idea of God, will grow stronger and bigger until His Wisdom will take charge of our entire life.

(5) *And she brought forth a man child, who was to rule all nations with a rod of iron: and her child was caught up unto God, and to his throne. (6) And the woman fled into the wilderness, where she hath a*

place prepared of God, that they should feed her there a thousand two hundred and threescore days. (7) And there was war in heaven: Michael and his angels fought against the dragon; and the dragon fought and his angels, (8) And prevailed not; neither was their place found any more in heaven.

The *woman fleeing into the wilderness* means that you go into the Secret Place within yourself where you walk and talk with God. There you live beyond time and space. You are in the silence, and to be alone in the silence is to be alone with God. God abides in the silence, Truth is lived in the silence, Truth is felt in the silence. You are in the Impregnable Fortress; no one can lay siege to you there. In your meditation and communion with God you will give birth to your ideal by knowing that what you claim and feel as true will come to pass in ways you know not of.

Michael and his angels who fought against the *dragon* (ignorance, fear, and superstition) represent your faith, confidence, and trust in the Almighty Power which brings all things to pass according to your belief. *Michael* represents moving concertedly in one way, one pointedness of vision, a complete and happy oneness with your highest good. When you pray, you call Michael and his angels; you gather your faculties and attitudes of mind and feast at the banquet table of God, rejoicing in the truth that God is the giver and the gift, and man is the receiver. With your sword of Truth, the clarity of thought, your understanding of God's law, you slay the dragon ruthlessly by chopping his head off with the fire of Divine Love and faith in God.

Chapter 13

(1) *And I stood upon the sand of the sea, and saw a beast rise up out of the sea, having seven heads and ten horns, and upon his horns ten crowns, and upon his heads the name of blasphemy. (2) And the beast which I saw was like unto a leopard, and his feet were as the feet of a bear, and his mouth as the mouth of a lion: and the dragon gave him his power, and his seat, and great authority. (3) And I saw one of his heads as it were wounded to death; and his deadly wound was healed: and all the world wondered after the beast. (4) And they worshipped the dragon which gave power to the beast: and they worshipped the beast, saying, Who is like unto the beast? who is able to make war with him?*

The *beast* mentioned here is the dragon representing all our negative moods, our old worldly beliefs, the old situations. The *dragon* works invertedly from the outside to the inside. The *ten horns* are the five senses doubled looking outward with limitation and at the same time impregnating us inwardly with what we hear, see, and feel on the outside. The *sea* is our undisciplined consciousness; our mind is chaotic and confused until we definitely define our goal, work toward a definite objective. We must feed the mind with premises that are true; we must dwell on ideas which heal, bless, inspire, elevate, and fill our soul with joy. We like to hold on to the old; the moment we get a desire for the new, we quarrel with it. This resistance to the new is the dragon which opposes the new idea in our mind. Limitation raises its head and our cherished ideal, enterprise, plan, project is wounded. We can and must heal the situation by casting out the old, accepting the new. This is the circle of consciousness where we die to the old and resurrect to the new.

(6) *And he opened his mouth in blasphemy against God, to blaspheme his name, and his tabernacle, and them that dwell in heaven.*

Blasphemy is irreverence toward, or refusal of, our good, or remorse over failure. We blaspheme against God when we say that God cannot heal the body which He created. At that moment we are atheistical because we are denying and rejecting the Omnipresence and Omnipotence of God. If a man says that he is incurable and that his condition is hopeless, he is blaspheming, in biblical language, because actually what he is saying is tantamount to the fact that the Infinite Healing Presence can't heal the diseased body, yet perhaps with his next breath he will say, "With God, all things are possible." We are also blaspheming the name of God when we say that God sends us sickness, disease, death, and trials. The Infinite Healing Presence cannot violate its own nature. The Infinite can only express itself as Harmony, Health, Peace, Joy, Wholeness, and Perfection. The nature of the Infinite is Wholeness, Beauty, and Unity. It cannot express itself in any other way. Life cannot wish death—that would be a contradiction of its own nature. God's will, intention, or purpose for all men is abundant life, joy, harmony, and marvelous experiences transcending his fondest dreams. The false beliefs of the race mind speak all manner of lies about God; men speak of devils, hell, damnation, limbo, and purgatory. All these words mean states of mind created by us due to ignorance and lack of understanding. The only devil is misunderstanding, misinterpretation, and misapplication of universal laws common to all men. To tell a lie about God and His qualities is also to blaspheme. To tell a person that God is going to judge him and punish him on the last day, or that if he commits a serious sin that he will go to hell is also to blaspheme. All judgment is given to the son, meaning is given to your own mind. You pass judgment on yourself every hour of the day by the thoughts you think and by your choices. The Absolute does not judge or condemn. Our retribution and reward are based on the reactions of our own subconscious mind to the way we think. Think good and good follows, think evil and evil follows. The law of life is action and reaction. Thought is action, and the reaction is the response from our subconscious based on the nature of our thought.

(8) *And all that dwell upon the earth shall worship him, whose names are not written in the book of life of the Lamb slain from the foundation of the world. (9) If any man have an ear, let him hear.*

The book of life has been previously referred to and represents the impressions made in consciousness; the *foundation* is the time when the impression is made. Consciousness is the *Lamb* which is always dying to the old and resurrecting to the new. As you detach yourself from the old state and feast on what you want to be, the old state dies and disintegrates and the objectification of your desire takes place. Verse eight means to listen to the truths within, know that God is All-Powerful and that He is the only Presence. Hear that love casts out hate, peace casts out pain, and joy casts out sorrow. Hear that there is only One Power and cease to give power to the phenomenalistic world. The scientific thinker does not consider an effect a cause; he does not give power to stars, weather, germs, people, conditions, or anything that is created or externalized. Likewise the one who hears believes and knows that Spirit is Omnipotent and the Only Cause. Many people hear only what they want to hear; they do not accept inwardly the truths they hear with their ears only, and consequently they do not live up to what they read and hear.

(11) *And I beheld another beast coming up out of the earth; and he had two horns like a lamb, and he spake as a dragon.*

The *Lamb* is a symbol of the savior state of consciousness. Our consciousness is always dying to one state as we give up our old beliefs and we give birth to the new. The correct way to use the mind is to take a true idea which heals, blesses, and inspires, and as we dwell on that idea it induces an emotion which weaves itself into the fabric of our mind, and it is brought to pass by the law of our subconscious mind. If you get lost in some aim, project, enterprise, you are absorbed, engrossed, and mentally and emotionally identified with your desire. This mental absorption conveys the plan or idea to the subconscious mind and it will come up as a lamb, as your savior, your answered prayer. But when you work invertedly from the outside, you are looking at conditions, obstacles, delays, impediments, and your subconscious takes these as your requests, and up comes limitation.

(18) *Here is wisdom. Let him that hath understanding count the number of the beast: for it is the number of a man; and his number is Six hundred threescore and six.*

This verse says that the beast and man are one. The letters in the Greek word *hephren* (undisciplined mind) add up to 666. This word means the lower mind, the unregenerate or undisciplined mind of man governed by fear, ignorance, and greed.

Chapter 14

(1) And I looked, and lo, a Lamb stood on the mount Sion, and with him an hundred forty and four thousand, having his Father's name written in their foreheads. (2) And I heard a voice from heaven, as the voice of many waters, and as the voice of a great thunder: and I heard the voice of harpers harping with their harps: (3) And they sung as it were a new song before the throne, and before the four beasts, and the elders: and no man could learn that song but the hundred and forty and four thousand, which were redeemed from the earth.

Sion means a high state of consciousness where high, lofty thoughts and ideals abide. It means that your mind is in tune with the Infinite and you sense the presence of peace, love, joy and spiritual strength. It means that you feel the Presence of God or good in your heart. *The one hundred forty-four thousand* represent the magnification or multiplication of your twelve faculties as you gather your thoughts, feelings, and mental attitudes together in contemplation of the King of kings within yourself. When you are tuned in mentally with the God-Self, you know that there is a solution to your problem. Every problem has its solution in the form of a desire. If you find yourself in the depths of despair or want, focus your attention on your ideal, picture yourself as free from the problem, believe that God is now working for you and that through His Wisdom you will reach your goal which will be your freedom. This is the *voice of heaven* mentioned in Verse two. A *voice* is a mood, tone, inner feeling which you possess as you stir up the gift of God within you.

The *voice of harpers* means the inner harmony which follows as you think of the power and the wisdom of God which is revealing to you the perfect solution. In verse three, you *sing a new song* when you sing the song of the triumphant spirit of God in man. No man can learn this song until he becomes aware of the Presence of God in his midst. You can start now to envision yourself as you would like to be irrespective of conditions or circumstances. Call your inner minstrel which is your faith in God and His Omnipotence, continue in this triumphant mental attitude, and you will rise from darkness and gloom and find yourself on the pathway to health, happiness, and peace.

(4) These are they which are not defiled with women; for they are virgins. These are they which follow the Lamb whithersoever he goeth. These were redeemed from among men, being the first-fruits unto God and to the Lamb.

Your mind is the eternal *virgin*, and you can keep it clean by refusing to unite with negative concepts, beliefs, and opinions. You follow the *lamb* or you become a bride of the church when you know that God's intention for you is life, liberty, and the pursuit of happiness. When you marry, *i.e.,* mentally and emotionally unite with harmony, health, peace, and wisdom, you are married to the lamb and you are a bride of Christ. All this means in figurative language is that you are constantly singing the song of triumph, achievement, and accomplishment of spiritual truth in your individual life.

(8) And there followed another angel, saying, Babylon is fallen, is fallen, that great city, because she made all nations drink of the wine of the wrath of her fornication. (9) And the third angel followed them, saying with a loud voice, If any man worship the beast and his image, and receive his mark in his forehead, or in his hand, (10) The same shall drink of the wine of the wrath of God, which is poured out without mixture into the cup of his indignation; and he shall be tormented with fire and brimstone in the presence of the holy angels, and in the presence of the Lamb.

Babylon in the Bible means mental confusion, a chaotic condition where we are in complete subjugation to sense evidence. *Wrath of God* has two meanings. If we think evil, evil follows, which is simply the law of action and reaction. If we impress our subconscious mind negatively, the law of our mind works destructively and inharmoniously for us. The wrath of God might with equal propriety be called the blessings of the Lord (Law). When we choose positive and constructive thoughts, there follows the destruction of limited and inferior thoughts and forms of life, culminated by a healing; the activity which precedes this healing is called the wrath of God, or the destruction of the old which is followed by the resurrection of the new. We worship the beast when we give attention to limitation of any kind, and create misery, sorrow, and suffering in our experience. The fire and brimstone mentioned in verse ten are figurative terms depicting the fires of conscience, remorse, revenge, fear, and despair which torment our soul for having wandered away from the Truth of Being.

(14) *And I looked, and behold a white cloud, and upon the cloud one sat like unto the Son of man, having on his head a golden crown, and in his hand a sharp sickle.*

The *white cloud* means the spiritual atmosphere generated by you as you look to the Spiritual Power as your Lord and Master knowing in your heart it is the only Power. As you lift up your ideal in your mind, you are ascending in consciousness, and through your spiritual thinking and confidence in God you become the Son of Man resurrecting your ideal and bringing it forth into manifestation. All that man has to do is to get a new estimate of himself and realize that he can become a spiritual paratrooper and fly over any obstacle, barrier, or difficulty to the haven of security, freedom, and peace. *I bore you on eagle's wings and brought you to myself. The sharp sickle* means you separate yourself from everything that denies what you want and impress your clarified concept in your deeper mind.

(18) *And another angel came out from the altar, which had power over fire; and cried with a loud cry to him that had the sharp sickle, saying, Thrust in thy sharp sickle, and gather the clusters of the vine of the earth: for her grapes are fully ripe.* (19) *And the angel thrust in his sickle into the earth, and gathered the vine of the earth, and cast it into the great winepress of the wrath of God.* (20) *And the winepress was trodden without the city, and blood came out of the winepress, even unto the horse bridles, by the space of a thousand and six hundred furlongs.*

When the grapes are fully ripe we press out the juice and make wine. *Wine* represents the new interpretation of life, the enthusiasm, joy, and exhilaration which follows our awareness of the Spiritual Power and the tremendous changes which can take place in our life based on this new idea. Wine is like blood, it gives life, animation, feeling. *When the winepress is trodden without the city,* we destroy our limitations, we give up our old way of life. Take your new concept, enterprise, plan, or purpose, pour the wine of life upon it by becoming enthusiastic, joyous, and full of expectancy. As you do this you are shedding your blood (life) or giving life, animation, and feeling to your concept, and it shall come to pass.

Chapter 15

(1) And I saw another sign in heaven, great and marvelous, seven angels having the seven last plagues; for in them is filled up the wrath of God. (2) And I saw as it were a sea of glass mingled with fire: and them that had gotten the victory over the beast, and over his image, and over his mark, and over the number of his name, stand on the sea of glass, having the harps of God. (3) And they sing the song of Moses the servant of God, and the song of the Lamb, saying, Great and marvellous are thy works, Lord God Almighty; just and true are thy ways, thou king of saints.

The *seven angels* and the *seven plagues* represent the seven stages of awareness or state of consciousness which have been previously discussed. The *sea of glass* means your mind at peace, and the *fire* represents the Wisdom of God which rises to the surface mind when it is still and quiet. The *song of Moses* means your capacity to draw out the Wisdom and Intelligence of God from your subjective depths which enables you to bring all your ideas to fruition. As you sustain the mood of confidence and faith, you will sing the song of triumph or victory of the spiritual power which is the song of the Lamb. This is the melody of God which you play on the strings of your heart which is the harp of God all the days of your life.

Chapter 16

(1) And I heard a great voice out of the temple saying to the seven angels, go your ways, and pour out the vials of the wrath of God upon the earth. (2) And the first went, and poured out his vial upon the earth; and there fell a noisome and grievous sore upon the men which had the mark of the beast, and upon them which worshipped his image. (3) And the second angel poured out his vial upon the sea; and it became as the blood of a dead man: and every living soul died in the sea. (4) And the third angel poured out his vial upon the rivers and fountains of waters; and they became blood.

Here we have a story similar to the plagues cast on Egypt mentioned in *Exodus* Chapter VII. This chapter refers to a reconditioning of consciousness. The vials mean consciousness pressing forth; they are the creative energies of consciousness. When we begin to recondition and purify our consciousness, we declare the Presence of God, and what is true of God is really true of man; but before this happens all our old race beliefs tend to hold us back.

Verse three says the sea became as blood. *Blood* is a symbol of life, and when we permit ignorance, fear, hatred, and superstition to rule us, we cannot drink of the waters of life such as inspiration, wisdom, and joy. In such negative states of consciousness we resist the influx of the Higher Life and we are dead to love, peace, happiness, and the wonders of life. As we continue to pray we will change all the negative patterns of the subconscious and a cleansing will take place.

(13) *And I saw three unclean spirits like frogs come out of the mouth of the dragon, and out of the mouth of the beast, and out of the mouth of the false prophet.*

The various verses in this chapter refer to the overcoming of various false beliefs, race concepts, complexes, and other poison pockets of the subconscious mind. The *frogs* mentioned in this verse are marsh leapers, they skip about. This represents an unsettled state. As the Truth comes into our mind, it creates a battle in our mind in order to resolve a conflict. The error is now on the way out and the Truth will conquer. The Truth comes to all of us as a sword. A sword severs us from the old and there are usually poignant partings as men wish to cling to the old ideas and traditional viewpoints of God and the universe.

(15) *Behold, I come as a thief. Blessed is he that watch-eth, and keepeth his garments, lest he walk naked, and they see his shame.* (16) *And he gathered them together into a place called in the Hebrew tongue Armageddon.*

The answer to your prayer always comes as a thief in the night. A thief comes when you do not expect him or when you are asleep. This is symbolic of the way the divine answer comes. It comes in ways you know not of and in an hour when you expect not. You *watch* and *keep your garments* when you walk in the light making it impossible for your prayer to fail. Your *garment* is your mood, your feeling, your attitude of mind. You watch and inspect all thoughts and ideas to see to it that they conform to the spiritual standard. You clothe all your ideas and true desires with imagination, faith, and confidence, and you will never walk naked in the sense of expressing lack, sadness, and suffering. The battle of *Armageddon* is always being fought. The battle is between what you are and what you want to be, between your lower self and higher self, between your spiritual aspirations and the race mind full of terrors and false beliefs, your desire and its opposite. Anger, fear, ill will breed antagonism, combativeness, and war. These mental poisons can be cast out by identifying yourself with the eternal verities and busying your mind with the concepts of harmony, health, peace, and good will. There will be a push and pull between these two forces within your own mind. Love, honesty, justice, and wisdom will prevail in this internal battle of yours. The only place where the battle of Armageddon is fought is in your own mind. As you practice the Presence of God, seeing God in all men and women, radiating His Love and walking in His Light, everything unlike God in your subconscious will be expunged and a Godlike man will appear; he will be the happy man, the joyous man, the healthy man full of Light and Love.

(17) *And the seventh angel poured out his vial into the air; and there came a great voice out of the temple of heaven, from the throne, saying, It is done.*

The *voice out of the temple* is the inner sound of the answered prayer, an inner silent knowing of the soul, the sabbath or rest in God. The *seventh vial* is the moment of complete mental acceptance or inner certitude which means there is nothing more to pray about for the mental and spiritual creative act is finished.

(21) *And there fell upon men a great hail out of heaven, every stone about the weight of a talent: and men blasphemed God because of the plague of the hail; for the plague thereof was exceeding great.*

Spring *rain* makes things grow. *Hail* is frozen rain and destroys vegetation. All our negative states are now frozen, withered, and destroyed by the Truth which enters into our mind.

Chapter 17

(1) And there came one of the seven angels which had the seven vials, and talked with me, saying unto me, Come hither; I will shew unto thee the judgment of the great whore that sitteth upon many waters: (2) With whom the kings of the earth have committed fornication, and the inhabitants of the earth have been made drunk with the wine of her fornication. (3) So he carried me away in the spirit into the wilderness: and I saw a woman sit upon a scarlet coloured beast, full of names of blasphemy, having seven heads and ten horns. (4) And the woman was arrayed in purple and scarlet colour, and decked with gold and precious stones and pearls, having a golden cup in her hand full of abominations and filthiness of her fornication: (5) And upon her forehead was written, MYSTERY, BABYLON THE GREAT, THE MOTHER OF HAR-LOTS AND ABOMINATIONS OF THE EARTH.

W̶e know our five senses of sight, hearing, touch, smell, and taste. The sixth and seventh senses are subjective. When we turn our attention within, we awaken the sixth sense which enables us to hear the goodness within, to listen to the glad tidings which are prophetic of that which is to come. The seventh sense is evidenced by our conviction or inner knowing that our prayer is answered. This interpretation is another way of explaining the seven angels. We can use our senses in two ways, for good or evil. We can turn our five senses inward toward the real and see, understand, feel, smell, and taste the Truth, or impregnate ourselves with all kinds of limitations.

In verse two, *fornication* means to cohabit mentally with negative or destructive thoughts and opinions such as hatred, ill will, jealousy, or resentment. The great harlot mentioned in verse five means the subconscious mind which gives itself to all and asks no questions. It does not argue with us but accepts as true what our conscious mind agrees with. You can impregnate your subconscious mind with all kinds of negative or positive imagery and it has no other recourse than to accept what is felt as true. The subconscious accepts without question what you feel as true.

The *scarlet colored beast* mentioned in verse three is the negative and perverted use of your mind; *woman* means your ruling emotions and attitudes which govern all the actions of your body. The body moves as it is affected by our emotions. It acts as it is acted upon. The woman (emotion) in us blasphemes when we reject our good and tell lies about God and His Love. The *harlot* is an adulterated, confused, neurotic state of mind. The *cup in her hand* symbolizes the subconscious which receives the impression of all our destructive or vicious thinking. The subconscious (*harlot*) is a recording machine which records all our mental responses, reactions, mental imagery, and habitual thinking. We can feed the subconscious with filthy thoughts or with marvelous psychological truths which have stood the test of time.

(8) *The beast that thou sawest was, and is not; and shall ascend out of the bottomless pit, and go into perdition: and they that dwell on the earth shall wonder, whose names were not written in the book of life from the foundation of the world, when they behold the beast that was, and is not, and yet is.*

The abyss or *bottomless pit* is negation. There is no ultimate reality to evil, it destroys itself. The only real evil in the world is the denial and rejection of the Presence, Power, and Wisdom of a God of Love enshrined in our own heart. All fear, hate, greed, and confusion of thought are really without foundation. There is no principle of fear, lies, jealousy, or hate, and not having reality, they must pass away. We can say that jealousy, hatred, ill will, animosity, poverty are facts, but love, peace, joy, faith, goodwill, confidence, loving-kindness, and abundance are the Truths of Being. We must distinguish between a fact and the Truth. We create a fact with our mind, but we cannot create the Truth. The Truth of God remains changeless and eternal. We can create discord in our mind, body, and environment, but Absolute Harmony is the Law of Being that never changes. *The beast that was, and is not, and yet is* means the denial of your good, your adversary. The moment you have a desire there arises in your mind opposition to that desire, a denial of it. For example, you desire to sell your home, the fear thought arises that times are bad, there is a depression, money is tight, etc. You desire to go to Europe and visit your son, but you cannot find the right person to manage your business, *etc.* You must meet this challenge in your mind and slay the beast which is the negative thought or fear in your mind, and permit your desire to live. Fear is a passing emotion trying to be something permanent. You rise above the obstacle in your mind and envision your good, knowing that what you contemplate and feel as true will come to pass. You know that you experience through your mind, and therefore you determine what you shall experience. You do not look upon circumstances and conditions as cause. Your mental conviction is the cause and the effect follows. This knowledge gives you faith, trust, and inner satisfaction.

(10) *And there are seven kings: five are fallen, and one is, and the other is not yet come; and when he cometh, he must continue a short space.*

The *seven kings* are the seven senses previously discussed in this chapter. *Five are fallen* mean that you are disciplining your five senses, the sixth is your ruling or dominant mental attitude, the seventh is the one to come—your conviction or complete mental acceptance. Whatever is impressed will be expressed. A conviction cannot be rescinded, it is a finished state of consciousness.

(14) *These shall make war with the Lamb, and the Lamb shall overcome them: for he is Lord of lords, and King of kings: and they that are with him are called, and chosen, and faithful.*

This verse is emphasizing what we have previously discussed, namely that whenever a desire arises in our consciousness, the beast (limitation) will come to remind or challenge us that we cannot accomplish, our peace is taken away until we cast out the beast. *He goeth into perdition* or dies due to lack of attention. You can starve any negative state by refusing to give it your attention; it dies because you refuse to feed or nourish it. Your attention gives life to all things in your world. They go into perdition when you practice feasting on your good in the House of God within you. The *Lamb* or your consciousness of the Presence of God is always the conqueror. Your faith in God will overcome all obstacles, set armies to flight, shut the mouths of lions, and do all manner of wonderful things.

Chapter 18

This chapter is an elaboration of the description of Babylon where materialism, sensuality, and judgment according to the five senses reign supreme. Buying and selling go on in the mind all day long. You can believe in misfortune, success, karma, that a jinx is following you, and you will experience all sorts of difficulties, troubles, and tragedies, for according to your belief is it done unto you. You can manufacture all kinds of junk in your mind such as remorse, self-condemnation, revenge, cynicism, ill will, *etc*. You are the owner, the manufacturer, distributor, and manager of this mental factory. You can this moment begin to liquidate all this junk which no one wants and begin to impress your mind with harmony, health, peace, joy, laughter, and the expectancy of the best, and the best will come to you. And you can make some good mental purchases such as accepting the fact that thoughts are things, that what you feel you attract, that your consciousness is the arbiter of your destiny and master of your fate.

Your state of consciousness is what you think, feel, believe, and give mental consent to. There is no other power or cause operating in your world. Purchase the idea that people, weather, germs, conditions, race mind, tradition, *etc.* have no power over you; that all these are suggestive only; and that the only Creative Power is your mind and spirit. Your thought causes the Spirit within you to condition itself in your world and take the form of your thought. Your thought and feeling create your destiny. Begin to practice these truths and realize that nothing affects you except through your thought. Someone might say to you that you will fail—that statement has no power except you think of failure. You reject it and say to yourself boldly and triumphantly, "I was born to succeed. God is always successful in all His undertakings, and so am I." From this you can see that no one has the power to hurt you. The Omnipotent One is within you. It is indivisible and moves as a unity.

The *city of Babylon* is an aggregation of negative thoughts, beliefs, opinions, and mental acceptances. The *kings of the earth* are the ruling egos of people or the dominant thoughts in our mind. You can get out of Babylon and destroy the city (your mental state of confusion) by practicing the truths we have set forth in this chapter. They are simple, direct, and to the point, and they work. Buy the right kind of merchandise such as wisdom, truth, beauty, guidance, and divine inspiration. You can sell this kind of merchandise to people everywhere and reap enormous dividends. Your profits from a spiritual, mental, and material standpoint will multiply exceedingly and you will discover the great truth that God supplies all your needs according to His riches in glory.

Chapter 19

(7) Let us be glad and rejoice, and give honour to him: for the marriage of the Lamb is come, and his wife hath made herself ready. (8) And to her was granted that she should be arrayed in fine linen, clean and white: for the fine linen is the righteousness of saints.

To be *arrayed in fine linen, clean and white* means that your garment or mood is one of goodness, truth, beauty, harmony, and good will. You must *wear the garment of God* which means the mood of love when you pray. You wear special clothes when you visit the President or the King. You must wear the proper mental attitude as you go to the King of Kings, the Lord of Lords, and the Prince of Peace within yourself. *The marriage of the Lamb* mentioned in verse seven takes place when you unite with your desire. The good that you seek is the marriage you wish to make. The *Lamb* is your good, the fulfillment of your desire. You must unite with your new conception of yourself. If you are seeking perfect health, that is the marriage of the Lamb. Your wife is your feeling, your emotional nature, which must be receptive to the Infinite Healing Presence. In order to get health, you do not dwell on symptoms, rather you withdraw the attention from the physical body and dwell on the fact that perfect health is yours now through the action of the Healing Presence which created all your organs and knows all its processes and functions. You remind yourself that disease or sickness is not outside the mind, but is manufactured by the mind, and in view of the fact that you can change your mind, then you can change the present condition. This knowledge fills your mind with faith and assurance. Continue to feel and know that the Healing Power is now responding to your thought, and your mind will be impressed by your assurances which increase in faith until your mind is at peace and joyous in its union with the feeling of perfect health and peace of mind. Your have performed the marriage ceremony in your mind because you succeeded mentally and emotionally in uniting with your good.

(16) *And he hath on his vesture and on his thigh a neme written, KING OF KINGS, AND LORD OF LORDS.*

This is a symbol of the creative act similar to the story of Jacob's thigh in Genesis Chapter Thirty-two.

And Jacob was left alone and there wrestled a man with him until the breaking of the day. And when he saw that he prevailed not against him, he touched the hollow of his thigh; and the hollow of Jacob's thigh was out of joint, as he wrestled with him.

The word *thigh* is an euphemistic expression meaning the creative parts of man. The ancients used phallic symbols to reveal great psychological truths. You are wrestling with an idea, you would like to become what you want to be, your reason and senses deny it and challenge you. When you reject the evidence of senses and feel that you are what you long to be, something goes out of you, you feel at peace, relaxed, and at ease. If you succeed in impregnating your deeper mind with your desire or idea, you become incapable of continuing to pray about it, as though it were a physical creative act. In other words, the mental and emotional creative act is finished and you are satisfied, and you no longer hunger or desire to pray. It is finished.

Chapter 20

(1) And I saw an angel come down from heaven, having the key of the bottomless pit and a great chain in his hand. (2) And he laid hold on the dragon, that old serpent, which is the Devil, and Satan, and bound him a thousand years, (3) And cast him into the bottomless pit, and shut him up, and set a seal upon him, that he should deceive the nations no more, till the thousand years should be fulfilled: and after that he must be loosed a little season.

The *devil*, our sense of lack, is chained but only for a time. When our desire arises, the devil or the negative aspect arises with it. The devil means living life backwards. If you spell *lived* backwards you have devil; if you spell *live* backwards, you have evil. The devil is our misunderstanding, our false concept of things. We see through a glass darkly;

in other words, we do not see as God sees. When you unite with your good, you overcome the sense of lack, and the devil or negation is loosed; but with every desire, a sense of lack will arise and challenge you for a time.

(5) *But the rest of the dead lived not again until the thousand years were finished. This is the first resurrection.*

The first death is the death of ignorance. We die to the false beliefs that we are victims of chance, fate, and coincidence, all of which are words used to denote our ignorance of laws of our own mind. We awaken to the truth that our own I AMness is God and that whatever we affix to the I AM we become.

(6) *Blessed and holy is he that hath part in the first resurrection: on such the second death hath no power, but they shall be priests of God and of Christ, and shall reign with him a thousand years.*

The first resurrection is going back to the Unconditioned Consciousness, realizing that whatever we claim and feel as true in the silence of our mind, the unconditioned will become conditioned accordingly. We have discovered the power of creation and we realize and know that the Almighty Power flows through our own thought pattern and mental imagery, and that we create the same way God creates. Our first resurrection is, the awareness of the Presence of God within us and our capacity to release the Hidden Splendor through our thought and imagery. *The second death* is simply the resurrection of our desire after we have overcome the sense of lack.

Chapter 21

(1) And I saw a new heaven and a new earth: for the first heaven and the first earth were passed away; and there was no more sea. (2) And I John saw the holy city, new Jerusalem, coming down from God out of heaven, prepared as a bride adorned for her husband. (3) And I heard a great voice out of heaven saying, Behold, the tabernacle of God is with men, and he will dwell with them, and they shall be his people, and God himself shall be with them, and be their God. (4) And God shall wipe away all tears from their eyes; and there shall be no more death, neither sorrow, nor crying, neither shall there be any more pain: for the former things are passed away.

Heaven means awareness. *Earth* means manifestation. Your new heaven is your new point of view, your new dimension of consciousness. When you begin to see spiritually, you realize that in the Abso-

lute all is Bliss, Harmony, Boundless Love, Infinite
Perfection, Infinite Wisdom, and Absolute Peace. As
you begin to identify yourself with these truths, the
sea or waves of fear, doubt, worry, and anxiety disappear, and your mind becomes peaceful, quiescent, full
of faith and confidence. You can now still your mind
and there claim, inwardly perceive, feel, and sense
God's river of peace flowing through your mind. You
are now in the Holy City—the New Jerusalem (your
mind at peace) characterized by such lovely qualities
as bliss, joy, faith, harmony, love, and good will. Your
mind is clothed with God's radiant beauty, and your
mood is exalted, noble, and Godlike. You are like a
bride adorned for her husband, as mentioned in verse
two, in the sense that you are married mentally and
spiritually to God and to all things good. You have on
your wedding garment because you are in tune with
the Infinite, and God's Eternal Verities constantly
impregnate your mind.

You also realize the truth of verse three, that you
are the tabernacle of God, for every man houses God.
Man's mind and spirit is the Presence of God in him.
God is Life, and God is all there is, therefore the Life
of God is the Life of man. His Holy Spirit saturates
and fills every part of your being. Every man is the
expression of God or the individualization of God
consciousness, another way of saying the same thing.

Verse four reminds you that when you realize the truth about God, you will come to the realization that God cannot be sick, God cannot die, be frustrated, suffer, or be sorrowful. You come to the conclusion it is all the illusion of suffering, sorrow, sighing, and pain. How could God suffer? How could God die? How could God learn anything? How could God travel? Begin now to claim that what is true of God is true of you and God will wipe away all tears from your eyes and you will experience no more sorrow, pain, sickness, sighing, or tears. You will find yourself God-intoxicated and seized with a divine frenzy. You have received the spiritual antidote which wipes away all tears from your eyes, and there shall be no more crying.

(4) *And he that sat upon the throne said, Behold, I make all things new, And he said unto me, Write: for these words are true and faithful.*

The *throne* mentioned is your own disciplined consciousness. You have the authority to separate the chaff from the wheat, the false from the true. Your spiritual awareness enables you to sit in judgment on all ideas, theories, concepts, and thoughts which come to your mind. Your decision is based on a spiritual yardstick of whatsoever things are true, lovely, just, and of good report. If any thoughts, concepts, or opinions do not conform to these, you reject them as unfit for the house of God, your own mind. You are now in the position to make all things new in your world because of your new estimates, blueprints, and postulates. All the mist and fog of the human mind dissolve in the sunshine of God's Love.

(6) *And he said unto me, It is done. I am Alpha and Omega, the beginning and the end. I will give unto him that is athirst of the fountain of the water of life freely.*

Alpha is our idea, our concept. *Omega* is the realization or manifestation of that idea. The oak is in the acorn, the apple is in the apple seed. If you dwell on your idea or meditate upon it, and think about it with genuine interest, you will find that the idea begins to master you and direct your actions according to the nature of the idea.

Whilst writing this chapter, I was interrupted by a long-distance telephone call from a girl in Paris who has been meditating on the idea of giving her talents over television. She said that she had received a contract a few hours ago and that she wanted to tell me about it. She wanted to express herself very much and had considered the idea positively and confidently; she had been nourishing the idea for a few months making it alive with her warmth and enthusiasm. The contract was simply a response to the working of the idea in her mind. When you feel the reality of the idea in the mind, the subconscious takes over and compels you to fulfill the role embraced by the idea. The beginning and the end are the same.

The seed has its own mathematics and mechanics within it, it has its own inherent vitality and process of unfoldment. The same is true of your idea, it has its power to manifest itself. In other words, the idea executes itself. The modern scientist working in a laboratory believes in the possibility of the execution of the idea. About one hundred years ago Dr. Phineas Quimby, a pioneer in the healing processes of the mind said, "I found that if I really believed a thing the effect would follow whether I was thinking of it or not." To believe means to accept the idea as true. Drop the seed (idea) in the fertile (receptive) soil of your mind and the Creative Intelligence locked in your subconscious depths will do the rest. You will then discover that alpha is your thought or idea, and omega is its objectification—that the two are the same, the beginning was the thought, and the end was its form, shape, and function.

(16) *And the city lieth foursquare, and the length is as large as the breadth: and he measured the city with the reed, twelve thousand furlongs. The length and the breadth and the height of it are equal.* (17) *And he measured the wall thereof, an hundred and forty and four cubits, according to the measure of a man, that is, of the angel.* (18) *And the building of the wall of it was of*

jasper: and the city was pure gold, like unto clear glass. (19) And the foundations of the wall of the city were garnished with all manner of precious stones. The first foundation was jasper; the second, sapphire; the third, a chalcedony; the fourth, an emerald; (20) The fifth, sardonyx; the sixth, sardius; the seventh, chrysolyte; the eighth, beryl; the ninth, a topaz; the tenth, a chrysoprasus; the eleventh, a jacinth; the twelfth, an amethyst.

The *city* is your consciousness, and *it lieth foursquare* means that man is the cube, a symbol of a perfect figure; the cube signifies a germ, an idea made flesh. The *cube* unfolded becomes a cross; the cross is symbolic of man's body. The *wall* is the radiance emanating from within and without us when we are at peace and full of His Light. *The twelve gates* and the *twelve precious stones* represent the twelve faculties or disciplines of mind. They are as follows: (1) perception, (2) faith, confidence, (3) righteous judgment, (4) love, (5) persistence, (6) disciplined imagination, (7) understanding, (8) desire, (9) discernment, (10) praise, gratitude, (11) zeal, inner hearing, (12) detachment.

When the Absolute becomes relative, it has crossed over from the formless to the limited state. This is called the crucifixion or crossing over from the invisible to the visible. Anytime you cross over from darkness to light, from pain to peace, from ignorance to wisdom, you have experienced a psychological crucifixion or crossing over from limitation to freedom. The walls measured one hundred forty four thousand cubits which means the multiplication and magnification of your twelve powers. As you begin to discipline your twelve faculties, you amplify, magnify your hearing, seeing, judgment, and all other faculties.

(21) *And the twelve gates were twelve pearls; every several gate was of one pearl: and the street of the city was pure gold, as it were transparent glass. (22) And I saw no temple therein: for the Lord God Almighty and the Lamb are the temple of it. (23) And the city had no need of the sun, neither of the moon, to shine in it: for the glory of God did lighten it, and the Lamb is the light thereof.*

Gold represents the Power of God and the Beauty of Holiness (wholeness). Man is the temple of the Living God. The day will come when you will no longer look to the outer temple, though necessary and essential to millions, but you will find the inner sanctuary. You will have no need for a building, music, incense, candles, statues, liturgy, ceremony, or ritual in order to remind you of God. The ceremonies and rituals in many instances tend to excite or hypnotize a person, giving the illusion that you are communing with God. You can be carried away by your five senses, and even influenced only by sight and sound. Prayer is an inner communion with God, a movement of the heart where you feel and taste the Lord, and find Him good.

Entering into the temple (your mind) has nothing to do with the five senses; you must shut the door of the five senses and commune with God in the silence of your soul and listen to the Divine Voice which speaks to the mind at peace. You do not need any props to touch God, you can contact the Divine Presence through your thought. Go into this inner temple now, meditate on the I AM, the Presence of God, think of all you know about God, and you will get lost in the joy and wonder of it all. You will realize that you are really Spirit and that you think, feel, and act as Spirit; there is no temple there, no shrine but the Infinite Intelligence of God is the light thereof. You are one with the Whole Spirit (Holy Spirit). His Spirit is your spirit, His Mind is your mind, His Peace is your peace, and His Love is your love. You have experienced the moment which lasts forever. You discover that beneath all the chaos, confusion, and strife in the world, there is an Ever Abiding Peace, Absolute Harmony, Indescribable Beauty and Bliss; you will sense that all men are one and that the streams of manyness flow back to the oneness. In meditation you move inwardly toward the Real, and as you go inward you realize first that this thing called the body is very unreal, and the earth upon which you are seated becomes unreal.

The external life becomes the dream and the internal life awakens and moves further and further inward; finally it seems to merge, and suddenly the meditating Self perceives that by going inward, it has found the Universe; that the sun, moon, stars, and planets are within. For the first time you know that planets are thoughts, that suns and moons are thoughts, and that your own consciousness is the realization which sustains them all, that temporarily in space are moving the dreams of the Dreamer; and the worlds, suns, and moons are thoughts of the Thinker. His eyes are closed and He is meditating, and we are His meditation. It is Consciousness meditating on the mysteries of Itself. This is the temple to which you go when you pray. It has no need of the sun or moon for the glory of God doth lighten it, and the Lamb (your I AMness) is the light thereof.

Chapter 22

(1) And he shewed me a pure river of water of life, clear as crystal, proceeding out of the throne of God and of the Lamb. (2) In the midst of the street of it, and on either side of the river, was there the tree of life, which bare twelve manner of fruits, and yielded her fruit every month; and the leaves of the tree were for the healing of the nations.

You can drink from the fountain which never runs dry. You can imbibe inspiration, joy, peace, love, and happiness. The Life Principle sustains the entire universe and feeds trillions of fish in the sea, birds in the air, and all animals on the land. His endless ocean of supply moves ceaselessly, tirelessly, endlessly, and copiously to all. Man must have a cup (an open mind), and receive God's blessings which are flowing through the river of mind to all men everywhere.

The *tree of life* is the Presence of God in you, and your twelve powers represent the *twelve fruits*. The Christmas tree is within you and all kinds of fruits are hanging thereon. Life is a gift unto you. You do not have to earn Life; Life or God was given to you when you were born, but you are to eat of the fruits of the tree, such fruits as peace, guidance, love, joy, goodness, truth, and beauty. All these, and many more, were given to you from the foundation of time. The leaves of the tree are the spiritual thoughts and values which bring harmony, health, and peace among all men.

(10) *And he saith unto me, Seal not the sayings of the prophecy of this book: for the time is at hand.* (11) *He that is unjust, let him be unjust still: and he which is filthy, let him be filthy still: and he that is righteous, let him be righteous still: and he that is holy, let him be holy still.*

Prophecy as you have already learned, is your own inner feeling, your faith, your mood which determines that which is to come. Whatever you are planning for the future, you are planning it now; the future is always your present thoughts made visible. Whatever you unite with mentally and emotionally is a prophecy of that which is to come. You are your own prophet. Be a true prophet, be a good prophet. Expect only good fortune and good fortune shall be yours. The children of misfortune are those who ascribe power to externals, other people, and the race mind. These are the only illegitimate children in the world.

In verse seven we are told that we must first change ourselves and then our world will change. Man is always trying to change the other person. Grant your relatives, friends, and all people their right to be different, grant them their peculiarities, idiosyncrasies, and religious viewpoints. Permit them to worship differently from yourself, be glad that there are Catholics, Jews, Protestants, Buddhists, and other religious bodies. If the other person is mean and nasty, that is no reason why you should be. You are here to let your light so shine before men that they will see your good works, thereby being a good example to all. Spend your time radiating the glory, beauty, and love of God, and never mind whether the other fellow does it or not. Change yourself, and as you change, your world will magically mould itself in the image and likeness of your concept of yourself. Identify yourself with the lovely, and you cannot see the unlovely. As your eyes are identified with beauty, you cannot see the ugly things in life. Fill your soul with love, and you will discover that love transcends all creeds and dogmas.

(16) *I Jesus have sent mine angel to testify unto you these things in the churches. I am the root and the offspring of David, and the bright and morning star.*

Jesus symbolizes your desire which is like the morning star which heralds the birth of the sun, which redeems the earth from darkness and gloom, and lights up the heavens with all its glory. Your desire heralds the birth of your savior also, for the realization of your desire would save you from any trouble be it what it may. Your desire is the root and offspring of David for *David* means God's Love, and your desire is Life's love to express Itself through you. It is God's promise in your heart telling you that you can rise and become that which you want to be. The *bright and morning star* is your inner conviction of your ability to accomplish whatever you undertake; this star or attitude of mind guides you and compels you to fulfill and bring forth the cherished desire of your heart.

(18) *For I testify unto every man that heareth the words of the prophecy of this book, If any man shall add unto these things, God shall add unto him the plagues that are written in this book:* (19) *And if any man shall take away from the words of the book of this prophecy, God shall take away his part out of the book of life, and out of the holy city, and from the things which are written in this book.*

It is interesting to note that in connection with these two verses of the Bible reference is made to the literary vandalism which was rampant in the days when the books of the Bible were written. It was customary to write them on parchment in the form of scrolls; however religious bigots and other unscrupulous persons often changed and expunged words and passages by interpolating forgeries. The letters of Paul and other parts of the *New Testament* have been known to be mutilated in this manner, but Bible scholars, philologists, and other research workers know where these forgeries are. There is no doubt but that religious sectarians were prevented from interfering with the contents of the book of Revelation inasmuch as they took the Bible literally, not realizing that its hidden meaning is the meat of the whole message. It is generally agreed that the text of this book of the Bible has been preserved intact through the centuries due to the fear of what men believed to be an imprecation. That is only the outer coat. The real meaning is something else altogether. Your word is your idea, thought, or formulated desire, it has its own method of expression as explained in a previous chapter. Your desire for wealth is a prophecy of that which is to come in the same way as a seed is a promise of a harvest.

Your desire for health, peace, true expression, or prosperity is the voice of God telling you that you can become or have all these things. Let us illustrate how man adds to the word of God; he prays for wealth and affirms that God is his source of supply and that His wealth is circulating in his experience now, and a few minutes later he begins to wonder how, when, where, and through what source his supply will come. He doesn't trust the Divine Source, and tries to help God. Man must learn that the ways of God are past finding out and that God has countless channels, and man's prayer may be answered in countless ways and in a manner that he knoweth not, and in an hour that he expecteth not.

I knew a man who was constantly praying for prosperity and looking to God as the real Source; and at the same time he was deeply resenting his employer because he did not give him an increase in his salary. This man did not really believe what he was affirming. Actually he was praying two ways, and like a soldier marking time, he was not getting any place. This man was double-minded and had a double allegiance. We must come to a clear cut decision and know that God is the Source of all our blessings and believe in our heart that whatever we claim as true, Spirit will respond accordingly for It is all things to all men.

The Creative Principle can prosper us in the same manner as It grows hair on our head or creates a blade of grass. It is all-wise and has the know-how of accomplishment. Man desires promotion; this desire is good and very good. Life is growth and his desire for advancement and expansion is the cosmic urge within him telling him to rise, transcend, grow, and express at higher levels. This is how he adds to the word; he looks around and says, "Well, that fellow is going to die some day, and I'll get his job." The desire was good but he contaminated and adulterated it. He should know that God can create another position like it and far better. Man doesn't want another man's job, he wants a position like it, with the same prestige, salary, etc. Infinite Intelligence has countless ways of bringing his request to pass. We don't have to hurt the hair of a living being to get ahead in life. Man must never undermine or hurt another in order to achieve his goal in life—to harm another in this way would be adding to the word, and *God shall add unto him the plagues that are written in this book;* which means that if we use the law negatively, we shall reap the results such as neurosis, frustration, sickness, dissatisfaction, *etc.* We take away from the word when we say, "I can't be that," or "I can't accomplish or achieve my goal." We are denying the Presence and Power of God saying God can't fulfill His promise.

Recently a man said to me that his boy was incurable. I pointed out to him that what he really was saying was that God couldn't heal the boy. He was shocked at his own statement and began to affirm that the Creative Intelligence which created his son could certainly restore him to harmony, health, and strength. A perfect healing took place curing the blood disorder.

A man came to see me about his son who wanted to go to college to be a physician, but the father said that he didn't have the money and that his boy was terribly depressed. The boy, in the meantime, compromised and went to work behind the soda fountain in a drug store becoming frightfully frustrated and unhappy. The father was taking from the word of God saying, "God could not open the way for my boy to become what he wants to be, so I'll get him a job somewhere." The plague that follows is man's failure to realize his desire which is the cause of all the hell and misery in the world. This father began to pray that Infinite Spirit would open up the way for his son to go to college, and he began to picture in his mind prior to sleep his son showing him his medical diploma which stated that he had graduated as a physician and surgeon. The father kept picturing this diploma and praying for guidance and right action. In a few weeks time an aunt died and bequeathed a large estate with ample funds for his son's education.

(20) *He which testifieth these things saith, Surely I come quickly. Amen. Even so, come, Lord Jesus,* (21) *The grace of our Lord Jesus Christ be with you all. Amen.*

The word *amen* means the synchronous union or agreement of your conscious and subconscious mind. There is no longer any doubt and your prayer is answered. The *Lord Jesus* is the Law of the I AM, and that law is *I AM that which I contemplate, I AM that which I feel myself to be.* You testify and bear witness to the truths of God by expressing His qualities and attributes and potencies in your mind, body, and circumstances. The Infinite responds quickly to your inner convictions and whole souled devotion and allegiance. Walk in the light or awareness that it is absolutely impossible for your prayer to fail; walk in the consciousness that the moment you ask, "It is done," and wonders will happen when you pray.

Verse twenty-one tells you that the I AM within you is the Christ or Savior, or the Law of the I AM is the solution to all your problems. Whatever you affix to the I AM, you become. You can now feel "I AM free," "I AM strong," "I AM illumined," *etc.*, and as you claim it and feel it, you become it. You have found your savior, for you are your own savior. The self of you is God. The law of God means the way God works. Whatever you meditate on, you become. Every day of our lives we must begin to meditate upon the beauty, the glory, and profundity of the Eternal One. Dwelling on the Eternal Verities within ourselves, we find an ever abiding peace which stretches out beyond the stars, beyond time and space.

When we are imbued with lofty ideals, when we think universal thoughts, little things disappear and all the petty things of life become inconsequential and are forgotten. Our soul actually becomes filled with the glory of the whole and the limitations, and restrictions of our daily life vanish. We find that this happy mood lifts us up and brings us *en rapport* with the Universal Mind of God. As greed, jealousy, discord, and other narrowing concepts which bind us to the wheel of pain disappear from our consciousness forgotten in the joy of Truth, we no longer are sons of man, but we become sons of God. We become one with the universal vistas. Constant meditation either in the woods, in your own home, or wherever you may be causes your soul to thrill as though touched by a divine harmony, and a pulsating, throbbing feeling pervades every part of you. It is as if the melody of the gods were played on your heart strings.

In conclusion, let us contemplate this profound truth, *Beloved, now are we the sons of God, and it doth not yet appear what we shall be: but we know that, when he shall appear, we shall be like him; for we shall see him as he is.* (I John 3:2.)

About the Author

A native of Ireland who resettled in America, Joseph
Murphy, Ph.D., D.D. (1898–1981) was a prolific and
widely admired New Thought minister and writer,
best known for his metaphysical classic, *The Power of
Your Subconscious Mind*, an international bestseller
since it first appeared on the self-help scene in 1963.
A popular speaker, Murphy lectured on both Ameri-
can coasts and in Europe, Asia, and South Africa. His
many books and pamphlets on the auto-suggestive
and metaphysical faculties of the human mind have
entered multiple editions—some of the most poignant
of which appear in this volume. Murphy is considered
one of the pioneering voices of affirmative-thinking
philosophy.

Printed in the USA
CPSIA information can be obtained
at www.ICGtesting.com
JSHW012033140824
68134JS00033B/3038

9 781722 501358